Reviewed by the
Parent-Teacher Advisory Board

Developmental Overview by Nancy Richard

becker & mayer!
BOOKS

A FIRESIDE BOOK
Published by Simon & Schuster

JENNIFER RICHARD JACOBSON

How Is My *Third Grader* Doing in School?

WHAT TO EXPECT AND HOW TO HELP

Fireside
Rockefeller Center
1230 Avenue of the Americas
New York, NY 10020

becker & mayer!
BOOKS

Produced by becker&mayer!
www.beckermayer.com

BOOK DESIGNED BY BARBARA MARKS

Assessment booklet designed by Heidi Baughman
Interior illustrations by Cary Pillo, Matt Hutnak, and Dan Minnick
becker&mayer! art director: Simon Sung
becker&mayer! editor: Jennifer Worick

Manufactured in the United States of America

1 3 5 7 9 10 8 6 4 2

Library of Congress Cataloging-in-Publication Data
Jacobson, Jennifer, date.
How is my third grader doing in school? : what to expect and how to help /
by Jennifer Richard Jacobson ; developmental overview by Nancy Richard.
p.   cm.
"Becker & Mayer! books."
Includes index.
1. Third grade (Education)—United States.   2. Education, Primary—Parent participation—United
States.   3. Parent-teacher relationships—United States.   4. Language arts (Primary)—United States.
5. Mathematics—Study and teaching (Primary)—United States.   I. Title.
LB1571 3rd.J33   1999
372.24'1—dc21   98-39750
                                                    CIP
ISBN 0-684-85718-9

Acknowledgments

I would like to give special thanks to my mentor and mother, Nancy Richard, who wrote the Developmental Overview for this book. Nancy has been a student of child development, school readiness, and effective classroom practices for the past thirty years. She has worked with thousands of teachers and parents throughout the country to promote classrooms that are educationally successful as well as responsive to the developmental needs of children. She has served on the National Lecture Staff of the Gesell Institute of Human Development, and has been a Consulting Teacher for the Northeast Foundation for Children. She coauthored the book *One Piece of the Puzzle: A School Readiness Manual.*

In addition, we would like to thank the members of our Parent Teacher Advisory Board, who volunteered countless hours to reading and critiquing the books in this series. They have graciously shared their educational knowledge and insight. Their wisdom, gathered through years of working with children in classrooms, has enriched these books tremendously. Their guidance has been invaluable. Members of the Parent Teacher Advisory Board are as follows:

Jim Grant, a former teacher and principal, is an internationally known consultant and one of America's most passionate advocates for children. He is the founder of the Society for Developmental Education, the nation's primary provider of staff development training for elementary teachers. He is also founder and coexecutive director of the National Alliance of Multiage Educators. He is the author of dozens of professional articles and educational materials, and his books—*"I Hate School!" Some Common Sense Answers for Educators & Parents Who Want to Know Why and What to Do About It, Retention and Its Prevention*, and *A Common Sense Guide to Multiage Practices*—are recognized resources for teachers, parents, and administrators.

Lee Ann Kennie, a specialist in child development, has taught kindergarten, first grade, second grade, and most recently, third grade for twenty-three years. She has developed curricula in language arts and science and is currently serving on a math task force with the goal of developing mathematical outcomes and benchmarks for her school district. Lee Ann coestablished, and for many years cochaired, Children's Literature Week at the Wilson School in Cumberland, Maine, in which children's book authors and students come together to share learning.

Mary Mercer Krogness, a public school teacher for over thirty years, is the recipient of the Martha Holden Jennings Master Teacher Award—the highest recognition the foundation bestows on a classroom teacher in Cleveland, Ohio. She has taught kindergarten through eighth grade in both urban and suburban schools and is currently a language arts consultant for five school systems, an educational speaker, and an author. In addition to award-winning articles, Mary is the author of *Just Teach Me, Mrs. K: Talking, Reading, and Writing with Resistant Adolescent Learners* and the writer/producer of the award-winning, nationally disseminated PBS television series *Tyger, Tyger Burning Bright*, a creative writing program for elementary-aged students.

Connie Plantz, an elementary school teacher for over twenty years, has had extensive experience with students of economic, academic, and cultural diversity. In addition to being a classroom teacher, she has held the titles of grade-level leader, reading specialist, teacher of gifted and talented students, and chairperson of the Multicultural Committee. She has developed curricula and acted as an educational consultant for homeschoolers and educational publishing companies; she has also taught graduate courses in reading and teacher education at National University in San Diego, California. Connie also reviews children's literature and is the author of fiction and nonfiction, including *Pacific Rim* for middle-grade readers.

Robert (Chip) Wood is the cofounder of the Northeast Foundation for Children, a nonprofit educational foundation whose mission is the improvement of education in elementary and middle schools. The foundation provides training, consultation, and professional development opportunities for teachers and administrators. It also operates a k-8 laboratory school for children and publishes articles and books (by teachers) for educators and parents. Chip has served NEFC as a classroom teacher, consultant, and executive director. He is the author of many professional articles and the book *Yardsticks: Children in the Classroom, Ages 4–14* and coauthor of *A Notebook for Teachers: Making Changes in the Elementary Curriculum.*

It takes many people to create a book. I would like to thank the talented staff at becker & mayer who produced this book, especially Jim Becker, who offered this idea; Andy Mayer, who has followed it through; Jennifer Worick, who graciously navigated this book through all channels; Simon Sung, who coordinated art; Heidi Baughman, who designed the assessment booklet; Jennifer Doyle, who worked with panel members; Matt Hutnak, who drew computer sketches; and Kelly Skudlarick, who worked on the original proposal.

I would also like to acknowledge the members of the Simon & Schuster publishing group, particularly Trish Todd, who has shared our vision and commitment to this series; Cherise Grant, who has been engaged in all aspects of production; Barbara Marks, who designed the book; Toni Rachiele, who shepherded it through production; and Marcela Landres, who did a little bit of everything.

I especially want to thank my coauthor on this series, Dottie Raymer. Although we have written separate pages, we have worked jointly every step of the way. Our philosophical discussions on education, teaching, and parenting have infused these books with words that represent our deepest convictions. It's been a wonderful collaboration.

And finally, I would like to thank the countless teachers, parents, and children who have offered their knowledge, anecdotes, insights, artwork, and advice. I hope you recognize your contributions on these pages.

—J. R. J.

For my parents,
who taught me to love learning

Contents

How is My Third Grader Doing in School?

Introduction

Your child has reached third grade. Are the days of block towers, blanket forts, and bathtub lemonade gone forever? They need not be.

It is, perhaps, unlikely that your eight- or nine-year-old will be reopening that bathtub lemonade stand anytime soon. Board games may replace blocks and clubhouses may replace blanket forts, but one thing remains constant: Third graders love to engage in play with their parents. In fact, third graders love being with their parents so much, they view almost any time spent together as play. This quality, among others, makes the third grade year an optimum one for giving your child a leg up in learning. It is a great time to help your child consolidate skills and approach new concepts with enthusiasm.

Research has shown time and time again that parent participation is a leading component of school success. Children from all socioeconomic backgrounds are happier, more motivated, and get better grades when their parents take an active role in helping them to learn. And there is no doubt that parents have advantages over teachers. For one, you have fewer children, so you have the opportunity to look closely at how your child learns. Does she learn best by examining things visually? Does she need to talk out loud as she works? What does she know about multiplication and what would help her to know more? Unlike the teacher, who must stick to an academic schedule, you can capture the "teachable moment" whenever it happens. Is she excited about a book she's just finished? Take a moment to find out what made this story so special. Is your child changing her room around? Help her to measure the furniture to determine whether a new arrangement will work as planned. And you have the luxury of learning while you help your child. It may have been some time since you've thought about the rules of syllabication or congruent figures, but relearning these things along with your child is a powerful exercise. It not only communicates to her that everyone, including you, is a learner, it also gives her a chance to see how someone else goes about solving a problem. When you are learning alongside your child, you bring your own energy and excitement to the task.

But . . . you protest. "We have so little time. My child may love being with me, but she also loves being with friends. And this is the year she signed up for every after-school activity available!" No doubt your schedule is too full to add a family "teaching time." So don't. Really. You don't need to add a structured learning time to your days. You simply need to use the time you already have with your child in a more creative manner. Approach the activities in this book as a way to add productive amusement to your days. You'll soon find that just engaging with your child in learning, with a spirit of curiosity and exploration, will add a new dimension to both your lives. In fact, just reading to your third grader every single day, if you're not already, will improve the quality of your own life as well as provide your child with an optimum learning experience.

This book comes with an observational assessment to help you determine what your child knows and what might be helpful to introduce to her next. This is not a standardized test. This is not an IQ test. This is not even a test in which the right answers are valued most. What makes this assessment ideal is that it gives you a window into how your child thinks about the subjects she is learning.

Consider nine-year-old Rachel's response to a question on a state exam. Rachel was asked to show an ABA pattern. She had recently moved from a private school to a public school and had never heard of this type of pattern before. Classmates may have written "green, red, green" to demonstrate knowledge of this pattern. Or perhaps they drew "hand, foot, hand." Rachel, on the other hand, began with what *she* knew. She drew a piano. She colored the pattern of black keys and white keys. She found and labeled middle C. From middle C, she located the keys that would play A and B notes. A pull-out from the piano and the "sounds" over the keys of A, B, and A represented an ABA pattern.

Will test interpreters accept Rachel's response as a correct answer? Who knows. But this one response is worth gold to an attentive teacher or parent. From this response we see that Rachel is a risk taker. She is not afraid to tackle a problem she has never seen before. Instead, she is confident in her ability to

Using ABA the notes creating a pattern makes an ABA pattern.

find a solution. It also demonstrates Rachel's awareness of patterns. She knows that patterns exist all around her. She's found patterns in music, and she will likely find number systems and their patterns familiar. The unexpected and creative response from the child is often more valuable than a "correct answer" alone.

As with all the books in this series, the learning activities in *How Is My Third Grader Doing in School?* cover the broad strokes of the third grade reading, writing, and math curriculum. Science, social studies, the arts, or physical education are not covered because the content in these subjects varies from school to school and cannot be presented accurately. Nevertheless, they are essential to a sound education, and your child needs to know that you value these subjects as well. Find out what your child is studying in these areas and see if there is a way you can contribute. Explore new knowledge in science and social studies, go to museums, attend concerts and plays. Discover how rewarding learning with your child can be.

Developmental Overview

by Nancy Richard

Talkative, full of energy, but sometimes needs to be reined in. Does this sound like your third grader? Perhaps and perhaps not. It is important to remember that while children within a grade will be around the same chronological age, each individual child will have his or her own rate of growth as well as pattern of growth. Some children grow quickly, others more slowly. Not all children in the third grade will be exactly alike, nor will they learn in the same way. Every child is unique. But because school laws dictate that third graders will be eight to nine years old at the beginning of the school year, nine to nine and a half at the end, the curriculum of third grade is geared toward a child of this age, and the general behavior of this age sets the tone for the classroom. A good teacher will understand this and will work with the developmental challenges of his or her third graders and use the children's strengths to help them learn.

A New Dimension

There is a wonderful payoff for anyone who can observe children at different grade levels. This person can readily see how children, their work, and their relationships are very different in different grades. One art teacher likes to tell the story of how she tried to get first graders to bring the sky down to the horizon. Because young children draw from their own perception of things—and not how adults think things are—these children were not happy about their teacher asking them to fill the page with sky. To them, this was not factual. To make her point, the teacher took the children over to the window and had them look out at distant fields. It was a bright sunny day with a very blue sky. And she showed them how the sky came right down and touched the ground. Seeing it with their own eyes, they agreed with her, albeit unhappily, and the teacher could see the inner conflict. Then one young man spoke up, saying, "Ugh ugh, it don't. I've been over there and it don't!" The children happily went back to drawing the ground at the bottom of the page and the sky on the top.

By the time they reach the third grade year, however, the artwork of most children changes dramatically. Gone are the tiny but detailed figures anchored to the ground with the sky above and the ground below, as if unrelated. Now the drawings fill the page; the sky comes down to meet the horizon; and there is a real attempt to show the third dimension and to capture perspective. Children in this grade change their perception of the world around them.

Third graders are confident and competent. Their thinking is original, expansive, and imaginative. Eight- to nine-year-olds love things that are new and different; they love challenges, and they will tackle anything. They want to do things for themselves, to work things out. But in their exuberance, they often bite off more than they can chew, and then get discouraged and give up. Children at this age need to be helped to take small steps, one thing at a time.

Relationships

It can be said that third grade is the year of relationships. Eight- to nine-year-olds are, above all, social beings. The introspection that so dominated second grade is gone; the third grader is reaching out to others: to family, friends, environment, and culture. And the quality of these relationships is usually very important to them. There is a new dimension here as well. Third graders are concerned with how others think, especially adults.

They watch the faces of adults for clues. They search the teacher's face and check out her body language, as if asking, How is she feeling today? Is she going to be critical? They intuitively absorb nuances of emotion. For this reason, it is crucial that adults be honest with this age group. Children can sense when words and body language don't match, and they will have difficulty sorting things out if they're getting mixed and confusing messages.

The third grader's relationship with his mother is especially intimate and intense. He likes being with her. He talks to her ceaselessly, and wants her to play games with him, to be involved in his activities. At school, the third grader identifies closely with his teacher. Her caring is very important to him. While he sometimes seems brash and abrasive, the third grader is as sensitive as his second grade self, and gets very out of sorts when criticized or when he thinks he's being criticized.

Another aspect of their maturation is that eight- to nine-year-olds measure themselves up against the standards of adults and society: They try to emulate adults. Still very sensitive, and now also self-critical, they can be hard on themselves when they don't meet these standards. And since they often don't have enough self-awareness to understand the cause of this inner turmoil, they may be uncooperative, sulky, or act out in negative ways.

What the third grader likes best of all is to be with friends. At school, the frequently heard lament is, "Can we *please* work together?" At home, it's, "Can I *please* have Juanita over?" Unlike the fickleness of second graders, who go from friend to friend daily, third graders like close friends. Some children want a lot of friends, while others prefer to have one good friend: a bosom buddy.

In school, the group is very important to third graders, and they like working together cooperatively, or with the whole class, in brainstorming or problem solving. They joke with each other, and the sillier the joke the better. Their zeal for life, their cockiness, and their silliness lead to boasting, bragging, and exaggeration.

In third grade, perhaps more than at any other time, learning the skills of interpersonal relationships—cooperation, mediation—is meaningful and very effective. Eight- to nine-year-olds thrive on the group process. Interpersonal problem-solving skills are as important to a child's success in school—*and life*—as are the skills of reading, writing, and mathematics.

Eight- to nine-year-olds are very aware of similarities and differences. They know how they are like their friends and how they are different. They will identify with, and often prefer to be with, people who are like them: those of the same sex; the same social and economic group; the same religious, racial, and national group. And this will lead to the painful exclusion of other children if it is not carefully addressed by adults. If parents and teachers approach differences in others with respect, curiosity, and excitement, third graders will respond with respect, acceptance, and eagerness to learn about these differences.

Naturally sensitive, third graders respond well to the idea of *respect*. They can identify with the hurt feelings that come with being left out or laughed at (even though they are often the perpetrators of such actions themselves). They are generally compassionate, and therefore ripe to develop more tolerant actions if these attitudes are insisted upon and modeled by the adults around them. And third graders are keenly aware of gender differences, and even have some budding sexual feelings. Because of this, they sometimes don't like to sit next to or be touched by a child of the opposite sex in play, or to be buddied as work partners at school. This, too, needs to be addressed. When this has been done, by the spring of the year girls and boys will be comfortable getting together in cross-gender groups to cheer each other on in games and schoolwork.

Cultural Awareness

Third graders often demonstrate a budding interest in family genealogy and traditions. They love to hear stories about when Mom and Dad were growing up, or their grandparents' stories about their mom and dad growing up. Helping your child draw her family tree (perhaps starting with stories about great-grandparents) and working down to her generation would be an activity she'd really enjoy. Done with art materials or needlework, this could end up being a very elaborate and beautiful piece of work.

Eight- to nine-year-olds also love family holidays and get-togethers. They like to listen to adults talk; they listen for family stories. They don't like to be "sent off" with the other children all the time. This is a great year to be included in family reunions that have activities, games, and sports with two or three generations doing things together. This balances their need to be competitive with the feelings of closeness and safety.

This love of culture also extends to the study of geography. However, third graders need to start their study of geography close to home, with the neighborhood and the community, before branching out to the country. They have only a beginning grasp of the world. You can help your third grader in her study of geography or history by starting with what she knows and helping her relate new information and understandings to herself and her own culture. You might also find books to read or videos to watch together. Discussing these with your child will help her to learn. While children can learn working alone, research has shown that they learn better when interacting with another person.

If you take your third grader on a trip, you can help her get the most out of it by discussing what she'll be doing and seeing ahead of time. If there will be a new climate, or new and different flowers, animals, or trees, help her to research this ahead of time. If you are driving, sharing a road map will add to her skills and knowledge. If she will be seeing people of another race or culture, help her to become acquainted with them ahead of time through research and literature. Bridging the known to the unknown makes the reality more exciting and adventurous.

This is a year that could be used most productively in looking at our country as multicultural and multiracial, and what that means for us as Americans. As this multicultural pattern continues to grow in our society, perhaps we need to ask the question, How do we relate to people of other cultures and other races? And, How do I want people of other cultures and other races to relate to me? There is perhaps no better time than third grade to begin to really probe these issues. At the end of the third grade year, when many of the children are nine to nine and a half, issues of fairness and man's inhumanity to man become very important, and they will appreciate having gone through this process.

Hardy, but Impulsive

Third graders live life with gusto. They seem to have inexhaustible energy even after a long day at school. They run in from school, drop their backpacks, wolf down their snack, and are out again to Rollerblade, play ball, or to a friend's house on their bikes. Because of this excess energy, they love relay races and running games, and have a passion for team sports like soccer and softball.

On weekends, if swimming is available, they'll stay in the water all day. In cold climates, they'll persist at skating and skiing until exhausted. Yet there is a negative side to all of this hardiness. Eight- to nine-year-olds are fearless and impulsive, and have a high incidence of accidents, often breaking bones. Because of this, parents need to set definite limits, especially around bikes and skates. Children won't set guidelines for themselves.

Active games and running play can help children of this age change gears after they've been concentrating in school for a period of time. Even just changing to a different kind of activity—perhaps one that is creative or involves moving around the room—helps them to stabilize.

Flightiness

Your child gets up on a Saturday morning planning to make some toast. As he runs down the stairs, dropping his pajama top on the way, he realizes this is Saturday, and his favorite cartoon is on. He turns on the TV, then decides he'll call a friend. In the kitchen, he remembers the toast and, still talking to his friend, begins reaching in the cupboard for bread. He gets out the butter and cinnamon, spilling some on the counter and floor in the process, then he goes back to his conversation. When you come on the scene, picking up his pajamas, turning off the TV, and seeing the mess in the kitchen, you wonder, What in the world is going on? There is a tendency at this grade level for children to overdo. They plan too much and then can't sort out the details. Their mercurial minds lead them from one thought to another, one activity to another, and they want to act on them immediately.

Because of this flightiness, third graders need lots of help structuring their activities. It's very difficult for them to clean their rooms without some organizational help. Like mushrooms, their collections seem to grow and grow, taking over the room. A good activity for you and your child to do together would be to discuss how his collections might be organized. As a starting point, you could say, for example, "What might be a good way to store your shell collection?" A trip to an office supply store or a store that sells organizers and household goods might give him ideas.

At school, teachers of third graders provide lots of structuring devices.

They have work-in-progress folders. They provide cubbies for things from home. They make charts for children that list what they have to do that day, and a column for checking off what they've done. They often set up a structure for getting homework done, perhaps designating a bright red file folder to be used exclusively for taking homework home and then back to school. You can help your child by making sure homework gets into the file and into the backpack before bedtime. If the teacher hasn't provided a special file for homework, you can provide one yourself.

Third graders love secret codes. Because of this, one way you can bring them back to the world when they're daydreaming or off the track is to have a secret code word that they've picked. When you use it, it means "refocus," "come back." Children of this age hate direct commands from adults, but using a secret word is "fun," especially when other people are around.

Dramatic Communication

Your third grader is dramatic! He rolls his eyes when talking with you or his friends; he gestures with his hands. He loves the whole idea of drama, and loves to make up and act out plays. One third grade teacher double casts a play each year. Each set of players puts on a performance for the other set. This gives everyone a chance, and they see how differently others interpret and play the characters.

At home, you think your third grader will never stop talking. He talks on and on in a loud voice with exaggerated and dramatic expressions. He tells you what happened to him that day down to the minutest detail. In fact, third graders are so enthusiastic about wanting to share their experiences that it is painful for them if you don't listen, or if you shut them down too quickly, or if you just don't have the time. While you probably don't appreciate or require *all* the details, you may want to store this sharing in your memory for those teenage years when you'd do anything for just a *little* communication.

Third Grade Split

Third grade has a unique distinction among the grades. This is the year when most children will move out of the thinking of early childhood and move into that of middle childhood. The split seems to happen about halfway through the year, as the children come into the nine- to nine-and-a-half-year-old range. Even though a new maturity of mind is very observable and wonderful, these "middles" need more than textbooks to learn. They still need lots of experience working with real materials and involvement with each other and the environment. Projects and field trips are important.

Another change occurs in many third graders after the split, though for some the change may not come until the beginning of the fourth grade. It is the appearance of a new, and usually negative, stage: an obsession with *fairness*. "It's not fair!" they'll lament. "The teacher is not fair!"

If you see your happy-go-lucky third grader turn into a whiner and complain all the time, or your once confident child into one who is timid and doubting, your first reaction will probably be to blame the school. In most cases, neither the school nor schoolmates (or you!) have anything to do with what is happening. It's just Mother Nature whipping up one of her turbulent growth storms. You need patience now. This, too, shall pass.

Firm and Fair

At school, one of the greatest tasks of the third grade teacher is to keep the class under control. Everyone wants to talk; no one wants to listen. The children can whirl themselves into a frenzy—talking, laughing, playing. They need a teacher who is tolerant of high energy but who is also firm and fair, who can set limits.

At home, one of the greatest tasks of the parents of third graders is to listen to them patiently. Another is to help them to order and structure their behavior, which often comes from lack of planning on their part, and a third is to help them to set limits and keep within boundaries. Third graders need parents who are firm and fair. Most of all, this is a year for parents to enjoy their gregarious, energetic, and creative children and to provide the understanding and trust they need as they approach the next stage of growth, and fourth grade.

Questions and Answers About Third Grade

I keep hearing about the new "critical math." We had new math when I was a kid and it was a failure. Why can't teachers simply teach the kids the skills they need?

By skills, you are probably referring to arithmetic or math computation. Third graders certainly need to know how to do computation, and yes, they need to memorize math facts, such as their multiplication tables. Few teachers will deny this. But just learning these procedures does not ensure that children will understand them or that they will recognize when they are needed. Third graders require many concrete, problem-solving experiences before they can truly grasp how numbers and functions work. Students who lack this experience often perform well as long as they can fill out drill worksheets, but they lose ground when they are expected to apply a genuine mathematical understanding to schoolwork and real-life situations. In order to have the skills they need, and to keep pace with mathematical learning internationally, children need to learn how to think mathematically, which is truly more challenging than just learning the tricks of computation.

My child has never been in a reading group before, but this year she's been placed in the lowest group. Should I be concerned?

Yes. Decades of research have shown that the disadvantages of grouping children according to ability seriously outweigh the advantages. Children in the lowest reading groups are often deprived of the company of good readers who model strategies such as rereading for self-correction or using the context to determine the meaning of words. They are often subjected to far too much isolated skill work and not enough reading. (Ironically, the children who need the most reading practice get the least.) And once a child is placed in a low reading group (euphemistically called the bluebirds or New Paths after the textbook used), she too often remains there throughout elementary school or for as long as the practice continues.

Aware of the detriments, many teachers now use "flexible grouping," which means they teach children in large groups and small groups. The small groups (sometimes called literature groups) are temporary and always changing. One week, all of the children who are interested in a particular author may meet and read as a group. Another week, random groups of children are brought together to talk about plot in the separate books they're reading. And, yes, sometimes children who need particular skill work or need to focus on specific reading strategies are brought together to learn. But no child is identified as a "dumb bluebird." If you are sure your child is placed in a long-term ability group, discuss your concerns with your child's teacher and, perhaps, the principal. The material "Reluctant or Struggling Readers" (page 101) and "Working with Your Child's Teacher" (page 188) may help.

My third grader is bringing home more homework than he can accomplish. How much should I be helping him?

Although no teacher expects parents to do a child's homework for him, a parent's guidance and occasional interaction can be tremendously helpful. Children at this age tend to procrastinate, have a short memory, and are easily distracted. No wonder third grade homework can become a trial for the whole family! If you haven't done so already, establish a specific time and place for homework to be done. If you can choose a time when you're available to orbit your child a bit, perhaps while preparing dinner or reading the newspaper, all the better. You can gently supervise and provide help as needed. Your presence will also communicate your interest and faith in his schoolwork. Third graders like company and are better able to stay focused when you're nearby.

Also, your child is still learning to take responsibility for getting her homework home and back to school. Do not underestimate this task. Make sure a part of each night's routine is getting homework into the backpack to be returned to school the next day.

Whether homework consists of measuring the rooms in your house or studying spelling words, your third grader is beginning to establish habits that will last throughout his school career. Here are some additional tips to make sure those habits are good ones.

- Ask your child's teacher for a consistent homework routine. If your child knows that spelling words always come home on Tuesday, then both you and he can plan accordingly.
- Give your child a special homework folder. Life would be simpler if children carried briefcases. As it is, papers stuffed into backpacks often arrive home crumpled and torn. A pocket folder with a big "Homework" label on the front can help homework get to and from school relatively intact.
- Don't expect your third grader to go to his room and do his homework. Even if your child doesn't need your help, he needs your presence. It does, however, help to give your child *one* place where homework is done. Clear off a section of a counter or turn the kitchen table over to homework for a scheduled amount of time each night.
- Make sure your third grader has all the tools he needs *in one place.* Your child needs to know where he can find a ruler or scissors or a stapler if he needs one. Many a third grader has been found sorting through baseball cards when he was supposed to be looking for an eraser!
- Teach your child to always read directions first. Homework is often done incorrectly because the directions were not followed.
- Hang a calendar in your child's room and show her how to mark weekly or long-term assignments on it. Even marking "spelling test" on every Friday will prepare her for the more complicated homework scheduling to come.
- Your child may need help breaking homework assignments into smaller parts. For instance, it's better to memorize four spelling words a night than twenty words the night before the spelling test.
- Help your third grader come up with a list of homework rules: How many times can he pop up and down to get himself a snack? Is TV allowed before, after, or during homework time? If the homework assignment is open-ended (like interviewing parents about their jobs), how long is he allowed to spend on it? Third graders need help beginning and ending things. A list of rules can give your third grader some of the assistance he needs.

If you put all of these routines in place, and your child is still unable to accomplish his homework, speak to his teacher. She may be able to make some adjustments.

My child is going to be in a class with another child who has severe learning disabilities. I'm afraid the teacher will spend all her time instructing this one child. How will my third grader, an average student, get her needs met?

Federal law now states that all children have a legal right to free, appropriate public education in the least restrictive environment. For many children, this means a place in the regular (as opposed to special education) classroom. Before "inclusion" occurs, however, the teacher, parents, and school specialists usually spend a good deal of time developing a plan that will support not only the child but the teacher and the other children in the classroom.

Children with disabilities benefit socially and academically from being in the regular classroom. It also demonstrates that other children can benefit from inclusion in the following ways:

- Children develop a greater understanding and awareness, particularly of the strengths, of people who are different from them.
- There is often another adult assigned to the classroom for part or all of the day. This adult, although primarily assigned to one student, often assists the other students in a variety of ways.

If you feel, however, that your child is not getting enough attention or instructional support, make an appointment to speak to your child's teacher.

I keep hearing about learning styles and different types of intelligence. What is this about?

Teachers who pay close attention to how their students learn can adapt their programs accordingly and give their students a greater chance for success. Parents who understand how their child learns can be more sympathetic with the frustrations the child faces in school and more helpful in finding alternative approaches. At the very least, parents need to know how to talk to their child's teachers. Some of the current thinking is described below. Remember, these classifications are not meant to label or pigeonhole children; rather, they are an attempt to understand how individuals learn best. Though your child (or you!) may lean toward one approach or another, most of us have a bit of each style within us.

Learning Styles

Imagine asking for directions at a gas station. The attendant tells you, "Go about a half mile down to County Route B then turn left onto County Route W.

Go about five miles until you come to the crossroads of Routes 116 and 47. Don't turn there. Keep going until you hit Highway 8. That's where you want to turn . . ." If you caught all that, you are definitely an auditory learner. If, on the other hand, you cried, "Wait! Show me on a map!" you probably learn better visually. There are three main learning styles:

- Auditory learners learn by listening. Show this kind of learner the fact 6 + 6 = 12 written on a page, and it probably doesn't mean a lot. Chant it, and it's in her head for life.
- Visual learners learn by seeing. This kind of learner needs to see to believe. Draw six stars and then six more stars on paper so that she can get a picture in her head.
- Kinesthetic or tactile learners learn by moving their bodies or by touching. Have this kind of learner build a six-block tower and add another six blocks right on top. If the tower holds up, she'll know her fact.

Multiple Intelligences

In the book *Frames of Mind: The Theory of Multiple Intelligence* (Basic Books), Dr. Howard Gardner describes eight ways in which people learn or approach problems. He has helped educators realize that *What matters is not how smart you are, it's how you are smart.* To teach a class the addition fact mentioned above (6 + 6 = 12), a teacher might offer a variety of tasks that take advantage of each type of intelligence. The eight intelligences described by Dr. Gardner and appropriate tasks for each are:

- Linguistic Intelligence: the ability to use and understand language in all its forms. Write a story about the addition fact.
- Logical-Mathematical Intelligence: the ability to use numbers and math concepts. Use pennies to show the fact.
- Visual-Spatial Intelligence: the ability to understand the relationships of images and figures in space. Draw a picture to show the fact.
- Musical-Rhythmic Intelligence: the ability to hear tone and pitch and to sense rhythm. Make up a rhyme or song about the fact.
- Bodily-Kinesthetic Intelligence: the ability to move with grace and strength. Hop along a number line to show the fact.
- Interpersonal Intelligence: the ability to work with other people and lead them. Work with a partner to come up with a way to show the fact.
- Intrapersonal Intelligence: the ability to understand one's own emotions, motivations, and goals. Think of a time when knowing the fact might come in handy in your own life.
- Naturalist Intelligence: the ability to understand things that exist in the natural world. Find an example of the fact in nature.

For more information about these educational theories, see:

- *Emotional Intelligence,* by Daniel Goleman (Bantam)
- *How Your Child Is Smart,* by Dawna Markova (Conary Press)
- *In Their Own Way: Discovering and Encouraging Your Child's Personal Learning Style,* by Thomas Armstrong (J.P. Tarcher)
- *Nurture by Nature,* by Paul D. Tieger and Barbara Barron-Tieger (Little, Brown)
- *Seven Pathways of Learning: Teaching Students and Parents About Multiple Intelligences,* by David Lazear (Zephyr Press)
- *Teaching Students to Read Through Their Individual Learning Styles,* by Marie Carbo, Rita Dunn, and Kenneth Dunn (Reston)
- *Unicorns Are Real,* by Barbara Meister Vitale (Warner)

How to Use This Book

Using the "Parent Observation Pages" and the "For Kids Only" Booklet.

Assessment is a natural process for parents. Every time you asked your young child a question—Can you say, Dada? Where is your nose? What color is this?—you were collecting information and using it to determine what to teach your child next. If you had questions about your child's development, you asked your pediatrician or consulted a checklist of developmental stages of learning. By observing your child and asking the right questions, you were able to support your child's learning.

Now that your child is of school age, however, it may be harder to maintain the role of supportive coach. It's a greater challenge to get a clear understanding of what is expected of your child. Without specific knowledge of the curriculum, you may not know what questions to ask. The purpose of this book, and of the accompanying assessment, is to help you observe your child with awareness again.

The word "assessment" comes from roots that mean "to sit beside." The informal assessment is a way for you to sit beside your child and collect the information you need. Once you have done this, you will be guided to activities that will encourage you and your child to learn together.

Keep in mind that the assessment is not a standardized test. It will not tell you how your child compares to other children in the nation. It will not even tell you how your child compares with your neighbor's child. But it will give you a starting point for determining how to increase your child's confidence and success in learning. Instructions for participating in the assessment are as follows:

1. **Take the "For Kids Only" booklet out of the envelope in the back of the book and read it through completely.** This will familiarize you with the visuals that you will be presenting to your child.

2. **Photocopy and read the "Parent Observation Pages" (page 37).** Reading these pages ahead of time will help you to see how the child's booklet and your instructions are coordinated. It will also allow you to decide how much of the assessment you want to give to your child at one sitting. Even if you think your child will be able to respond to most of these questions, you will want to give the three parts of the assessment (math, writing, and reading) at different times. You may even decide to divide the three parts into even smaller sections to accommodate your child's attention span or your particular time schedule.

3. **Provide a place to give the assessment that is relatively free of distractions.** Talk to your third grader about the activities. Tell your child that you want to learn more about him and that these activities will teach *you.* Make sure you approach the activity in a lighthearted manner.

4. **Above all, keep the assessment fun and relaxed for your child.** If your child is afraid to try an activity, don't push him. After all, that is also valuable information for you. Whenever your child has difficulty with a reading passage or a math problem, *stop* and skip ahead to the question directed. There is never a reason to work beyond your child's comfort level.

5. **Give positive reinforcement as often as possible.** You might just say, "I didn't know you could do that!" If your child seems upset or confused by an exercise, let him off the hook. You might say, "That question is real confusing, isn't it?" Make sure your child ends the assessment feeling successful. One way of doing this is to return to a question your child could answer with obvious ease. Say, "I forgot to write your answer down. Can you show me how you did this problem again?"

Using the Assessment Guide

The "Assessment Guide" (page 56) will help you to figure out what your child knows and what he is ready to learn next. If a question on the assessment did not give you enough information, or if you are confused about your child's response, you may want to talk to your child's teacher. See page 188 for more information.

Using the Suggested Activities

In each skill area, activities are suggested under two headings: "Have Five Minutes?" and "Have More Time?" Some of the activities in the five-minute section are quick games that you and your child can play while waiting for dinner, riding in the car, or walking to the bus stop. Others are activities that you can explain in less than five minutes and then let your child complete on his own. Activities in the "Have More Time?" category require more planning or a longer time commitment on your part.

Do not feel that you should do every activity listed under a skill heading. A number of different activities are provided so you can pick and choose the ones that appeal to you and your child. And don't feel guilty if you haven't tried something new for a while. If you do only a couple of these activities occasionally, you will be giving your third grader a genuine boost toward success. You'll be amazed at how a question here and a three-minute activity there can demonstrate to your child how much you value his ideas and his education. Feel free to adapt these activities to your needs.

Even if you are not directed to a specific section, you may want to try some of the activities there anyway. Reviewing has wonderful benefits. When your child revisits a skill, he usually gains a deeper understanding that he can then apply to new learning. In every area there are sure to be games your child will enjoy playing.

Should you pursue activities that seem more difficult? Probably not. Pushing your child too fast may backfire. Instead of looking forward to the games you initiate, your child may associate them with confusion, boredom, or failure. It's good to remember that success is the greatest motivator of all.

Some of the activities are competitive. Some third graders do not care for competitive games. If your child is one, make the activity noncompetitive. Rather than playing against each other, make yourselves a team and try to beat the clock or an imaginary player—who always makes the most ridiculous decisions!

Reassess

Repeat the assessment when appropriate.

After some time has gone by—perhaps two or three months—and you and your child have participated in many of the activities, you may want to give the assessment, or a portion of it, again. By reassessing, you can determine if your child has grown in his understanding of concepts. It's possible that the "Assessment Guide" (page 56) will direct you to new areas of learning to focus on next.

If you choose not to give the entire assessment a second time, make sure you ask some questions that you know your child will answer competently. *Always end the assessment on a positive note.*

Remember, the assessment is meant to be an informal tool for gathering information. You may want to adapt the questions or ask new ones to see if your third grader has truly mastered a skill.

Many teachers now assess children in the classroom by doing what one educator termed "kid watching." This is what parents have always done best. Have a ball watching your child grasp new knowledge.

Parent Observation Pages

Photocopy the "Parent Observation Pages." This will allow you to match your child's responses to the answer guide more easily. It will also allow you to repeat the assessment with your child or to give the assessment to a sibling.

Ask your child the questions that appear throughout the assessment. Do not feel, however, that you must rigidly adhere to the wording. These questions are meant to be a guide, not a script. You may find other ways of questioning that are more suited to your own and your child's needs. For more information, see "How to Use This Book," page 33.

Reading Assessment

Use assessment booklet pages 2–3 for questions 1 and 2.

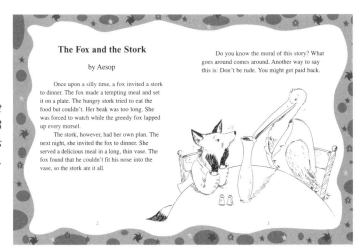

The Fox and the Stork

by Aesop

Once upon a silly time, a fox invited a stork to dinner. The fox made a tempting meal and set it on a plate. The hungry stork tried to eat the food but couldn't. Her beak was too long. She was forced to watch while the greedy fox lapped up every morsel.

The stork, however, had her own plan. The next night, she invited the fox to dinner. She served a delicious meal in a long, thin vase. The fox found that he couldn't fit his nose into the vase, so the stork ate it all.

Do you know the moral of this story? What goes around comes around. Another way to say this is: Don't be rude. You might get paid back.

1. **Use pages 2 and 3 of the booklet.** Ask your child, *Can you read this story?* If your child stops at a word, give him or her a moment to figure it out, then supply the word if necessary.

   What does your child do to figure out a word he or she doesn't know? Check all that apply.

   ___ Sounds it out
   ___ Divides the word into syllables
   ___ Guesses based on context
   ___ Skips the word and then goes back
   ___ Looks at the picture
   ___ Knew all the words

2. Can your child answer these questions? Check all **correct** answers.

   ___ A. What happened in this story? (Your child should be able to retell the story in correct order.)
   ___ B. Why did the Stork serve dinner in the tall vase? (She wanted to treat the fox the way she was treated.)
   ___ C. What does the word "morsel" mean? (A bite of food. Your child should be able to make a close guess based on the context.)
   ___ D. Do you think the stork's plan was a good one? Why or why not? (Check if your child evaluated the stork's plan.)

*I*f your child stopped at five or more words in the story, STOP HERE and go to question 5.

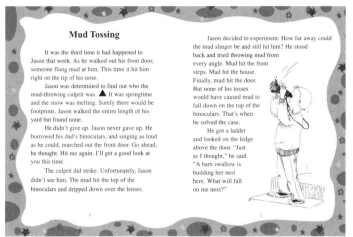

Use assessment booklet pages 4–5 for questions 3 and 4.

3. **Use pages 4 and 5 of the booklet.** If your child stopped at fewer than five words, ask, *Can you read this story to here?* (point to the black triangle). If your child stops at a word, give him or her a moment to figure it out, then supply the word if necessary.
   When your child reaches the triangle, ask, *What do you think will happen next?* Check one.
   ___ makes a prediction
   ___ does not make a prediction

4. *Continue reading so we can see what happens.*
   Can your child answer these questions? Check all **correct** answers.
   ___ A. Can you tell me, in just a few sentences, what happened in this story? (Jason thought someone was throwing mud at him. As it turned out, a swallow was building a mud nest above the door.)
   ___ B. What is a culprit? (A person who is guilty of doing something wrong.)
   ___ C. What do barn swallows use to build their nests? (mud) How do you know? (Because mud dropped when the bird was building.)
   ___ D. How are Jason and the stork from the last story the same? How are they different? (Accept reasonable responses.)

___ E. What would you have done if you were Jason? (Check if your child tries to answer.)

___ F. Springtime and footsteps are compound words. Can you think of any other compound words? (Accept any words that are formed by combining two words.)

___ G. Can you pick out three synonyms (words that have almost the same meaning) in this story? (tossing and throwing, walked and marched, hit and strike are possible answers.)

> If your child stopped at five or more words in the previous story, go to questions 5 and 6. Then proceed to question 8 (skip 7).

Use assessment booklet pages 6–7 for questions 5 and 6.

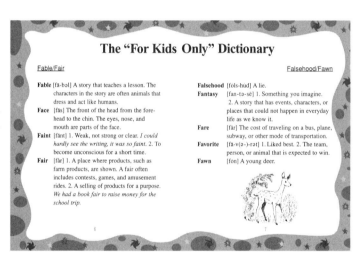

5. **Use pages 6 and 7 of the booklet.** *Here is a dictionary scavenger hunt. Let's see how many questions you can answer.*

6. Can your child find the answers to these questions? Check all **correct** responses.

___ A. Which word means a lie? (falsehood)

___ B. Can you find a pair of homonyms? (fair, fare) (If your child does not know what the word "homonyms" mean, say, "Homonyms are words that sound alike but are spelled differently and have different meanings.")

___ C. Can you tell me two words that have three syllables? (fantasy, favorite)

___ D. Can you think of a word that could appear between the words face and faint? (A correct word would fit according to alphabetical order.)

___ E. What are the guidewords on the page where the word "face" can be found? (fable, fair)

___ F. What are the two meanings of faint? (weak, become unconscious)

If your child stopped at five or more words in "Mud Tossing," proceed to question 8.

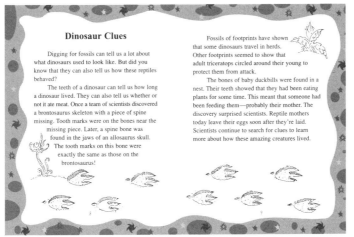

Use assessment booklet pages 8–9 for questions 7 and 8.

7. **Use pages 8 and 9 of the booklet.** If your child could read "Mud Tossing" without stopping at five or more words, ask, *Can you read this article?* If your child stops at a word, give him or her a moment to figure it out, then supply the word if necessary.

Can your child answer these questions? Check all **correct** answers.

___ A. What is the main idea of this article? (Fossils can tell us how dinosaurs behaved.)

___ B. What are the details that support the main idea? (Teeth can indicate the age and diet of a dinosaur, footprints and bones can indicate how dinosaurs worked together and cared for one another.)

___ C. What do you think happened to the brontosaurus? (the allosaurus ate the brontosaurus *or* the brontosaurus died and then the allosaurus ate it.)

___ D. Is this article fiction or nonfiction? (nonfiction)

___ E. If you wanted to find more information about dinosaurs, where would you look? If your child answers, "the library," ask, "Where would you look in the library?" (Correct responses might include: the card catalog, the computer catalog, encyclopedia, or Internet, the nonfiction shelves, the encyclopedia, specific books your child is familiar with, or asking an expert.)

8. What are your child's reading habits? Check all that apply.

___ Listens to me or another adult read on a regular basis

___ Reads to him- or herself daily

___ Is interested in a wide range of reading materials (nonfiction, fiction, magazines)

___ Searches books or magazines for answers to questions

___ Likes to predict what will happen in a story

___ Talks about a story as he or she reads it or when the story is completed

Writing Assessment

Use assessment booklet pages 10–11 for question 1.

Have your child read and follow the directions on pages 10 and 11 of the "For Kids Only" booklet. (Have paper and pencil available for your child to use.)

1. Does your child's letter show the following? (Check all that apply.)
    ___ A. Approached this writing task with confidence
    ___ B. Considered the audience when writing (the pen pal)
    ___ C. Expresses ideas clearly and in logical sequence
    ___ D. Writes complete sentences
    ___ E. Uses the five parts of a letter: date, greeting, body, closing, signature
    ___ F. Avoids run-on sentences (These are long sentences that could be divided into a number of shorter sentences. Run-on sentences usually contain too many "ands" or "buts.")
    ___ G. Uses paragraph form
    ___ H. Paragraphs begin with a topic sentence and are followed by supporting details
    ___ I. Uses capitalization and punctuation properly
    ___ J. Uses conventional spelling 70 to 90 percent of the time
    ___ K. Takes risks by using words that may or may not be spelled correctly
    ___ L. Uses cursive writing

*Use assessment
booklet pages
12–13.*

All About You

Do you like to write?

Yes, because _____

No, because _____

There are lots of different types of writing. Give each of the types of writing below a number. Here are what the numbers mean:

1 - I love to write these.
2 - Sometimes I like to write these.
3 - I hate to write these.
4 - I never tried writing these before.

___ stories   ___ reports   ___ personal essays
___ poems   ___ letters

Have you ever done research before? ___ yes ___ no

Where would you look for information if you were going to write about taking care of pets?

_____
_____
_____

12

The best thing I ever wrote was _____

_____

because _____.

The worst thing I ever wrote was _____

because _____.

I wish I were better at _____

_____

Are you a good speller?
___ very good   ___ not very good
___ okay   ___ terrible

Have you ever given a presentation before?
___ yes ___ no

If yes, check which kind:
___ book report
___ science or social studies report
___ other

Are you tired of answering all these questions?
___ yes ___ no

13

The "All About You" survey on pages 12 and 13 of the booklet will also help you to assess your child's knowledge, comfort level, and needs when it comes to writing. You will want to have it handy when using the "Assessment Guide" (page 56).

Math Assessment

Before beginning the math assessment, have paper and pencil available for your child to use. You may also wish to have a calculator to check your child's computation and a watch with a second hand (see question 5). If your child has difficulty reading any of the math problems in the "For Kids Only" booklet, go ahead and read the passages aloud.

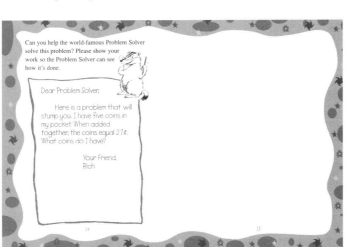

Use assessment booklet pages 14–15 for question 1.

1. **Use pages 14 and 15 of the booklet.** *Can you solve this problem?*
   Remember to show your work.
   Check all that apply.
   ___ A. Read and understood the problem
   ___ B. Came up with a plan for solving the problem
   ___ C. Expressed confidence (or seemed confident) while attempting to solve the problem
   ___ D. Used one or more of the following strategies:
   (Check one or more)
   ___ used objects
   ___ drew a picture
   ___ made a chart
   ___ made an organized list
   ___ looked for a pattern
   ___ worked backwards
   ___ thought of a simpler problem
   ___ guessed and checked
   ___ used logical reasoning

___ E. Persisted until a solution was found

___ F. Found the correct solution to the problem (two dimes, one nickel, two pennies)

___ G. Checked the accuracy of the solution without prompting

___ H. Understood the value of coins

___ I. Was able to add coin values successfully

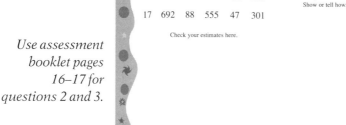

Use assessment booklet pages 16–17 for questions 2 and 3.

Inside image:

26   168   54   33   436   208

17   692   88   555   47   301

Check your estimates here.

Can you check one of your estimates another way? Show or tell how.

16   17

2. **Use pages 16 and 17 of the booklet.** *I'm going to ask you to estimate. Point to the numbers that make the most sense.*

   • *Which two numbers, when added, would equal a number close to 100?* (Wait for a response.)
   Now check your guess. (You may want to use a calculator to check your child's response.) Check one in each row.
      ___ Estimate was within 20
      ___ Difference between your child's guess and the actual number was above 20
      ___ Added correctly to check estimate
      ___ Did not add correctly

   • *Which two numbers, when added, would equal a number close to 450?* (Wait for a response.)
   Now check your guess. Check one in each row.
      ___ Estimate was within 20
      ___ Difference was above 20

___ Added correctly to check estimate
___ Did not add correctly

- *Which two numbers, when subtracted, would equal a number close to 29?* (Wait for a response.)
  Now check your guess. Check all that apply.
    ___ Estimate was within 20
    ___ Difference was above 20
    ___ Subtracted correctly to check estimate
    ___ Did not subtract correctly

- *Which two numbers, when subtracted, would equal a number close to 500?* (Wait for a response.)
  Now check your guess. Check all that apply.
    ___ Estimate was within 20
    ___ Difference was above 20
    ___ Subtracted correctly to check estimate
    ___ Did not subtract correctly

- *Which three numbers, when added, would equal a number close to 1,000?* (Wait for a response.)
  Now check your guess. Check all that apply.
    ___ Estimate was within 30
    ___ Difference was above 30
    ___ Added correctly to check estimate
    ___ Did not add correctly

3. Was your child able to show another way of checking one of his or her estimates?
    ___ Yes
    ___ No

Use assessment booklet pages 18–19 for questions 4 and 5.

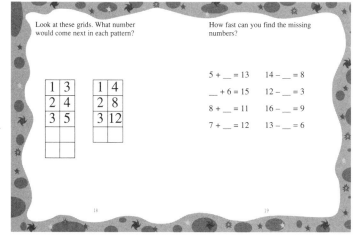

Look at these grids. What number would come next in each pattern?

1	3
2	4
3	5

1	4
2	8
3	12

How fast can you find the missing numbers?

5 + __ = 13   14 − __ = 8

__ + 6 = 15   12 − __ = 3

8 + __ = 11   16 − __ = 9

7 + __ = 12   13 − __ = 6

18   19

4. **Use page 18 of the booklet.** *What numbers come next in each grid?* Check all that apply.
   ___ Gave the correct response for grid a (4, 6, 5, 7)
   ___ Gave the correct response for grid b (4, 16)
   ___ Could not fill in the grids at this time

5. **Use page 19 of the booklet.** *How many of these sentences can you complete in one minute?* Time your third grader. Say "Stop" when a minute has passed.
   Check all that apply.
   ___ Cannot complete these problems at this time
   ___ Completed some of the sentences correctly in the time allotted
   ___ Completed all of the sentences in the time allotted but made errors
   ___ Completed the sentences correctly in less than one minute

*Use assessment
booklet pages
20–21 for
questions 6 to 8.*

6. **Use page 20 of the booklet.** *What shape is this in the center of the graph
paper?* (rectangle) *Can you tell me the area of this rectangle? Can you tell me
the perimeter of the rectangle?*
Check all that apply.
___ Named the rectangle
___ Determined the area of the rectangle (12 squares)
___ Determined the perimeter of the rectangle (14 sides of squares)
___ Has not been introduced to area or perimeter yet

7. **Use page 21 of the booklet.** *If I sent you to this stand to buy a gallon of
lemonade, which container would you buy?*
Check one.
___ Pointed to figure d (correct response)
___ Does not know gallon at this time

8. *What if the stand was all out of gallon containers, but you knew that I
needed to have that amount. Is there anything you could do?* (Wait for a
response) *Is there another way that you could buy the same amount of
lemonade?* (Again, wait for a response) *Any others?* Check one.
___ Gave any of the following correct responses:
two half gallons (figure b)
four quart containers (figure c)
one half gallon, two quarts
eight pints (figure a)
four pints, one half gallon
two pints, one quart, one half gallon
two pints, three quarts

___ Gave two correct responses
___ Gave three or more correct responses
___ Has not developed an understanding of capacity yet
___ Was not able to combine containers to reach the appropriate amount

*Use assessment
booklet pages
22–23 for
questions 9 to 13.*

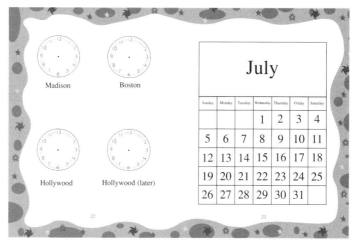

9. **Use page 22 of the booklet.** *It is 10:36 A.M. in Madison, Wisconsin. Can you show that time on the Madison clock?* Check one.
   ___ Draws hands correctly to the minute
   ___ Draws the time to the minute but confuses the hour and minute hand
   ___ Cannot draw the time to the minute at this time

10. *It is one hour later in Boston, Massachusetts. Can you show the correct time on the Boston clock?* Check one.
    ___ Draws the hands to show 11:36
    ___ Shows 11:36 but confuses the hands
    ___ Does not add an hour correctly
    ___ Cannot draw the time to the minute at this time

11. *It is two hours earlier in Hollywood, California, than it is in Madison. Can you draw the correct time in Hollywood?* Check one.
    ___ Draws the hands to show 8:36
    ___ Shows 8:36 but confuses the hands
    ___ Does not subtract the hours correctly
    ___ Cannot draw the time to the minute at this time

12. *What time will it be in Hollywood twenty-four minutes from now?*
___ Draws the hands to show 9:00 A.M.
___ Shows 9:00 but confuses the hands
___ Does not add the minutes correctly
___ Cannot draw the time to the minute at this time

13. **Use page 23 of the booklet.** *Look at the calendar page to answer these questions.*
- *How many weeks are there in July?* (five or four and a half)
- *What day of the week is July 4?* (Saturday)
- *If today was July 11, how many days would it be until July 26?* (15)
- *What date will come after July 31?* (August 1)

Check one.
___ Could answer all of these questions at this time
___ Could not answer all of these questions at this time

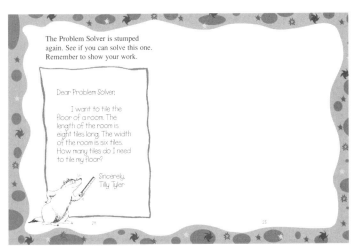

Use assessment booklet pages 24–25 for question 14.

14. **Use page 24 of the booklet.** *Can you solve this problem? Remember, show your work.*
Check all that apply.
___ A. Read and understood the problem
___ B. Came up with a plan for solving the problem
___ C. Expressed confidence (or seemed confident) while attempting to solve the problem
___ D. Used one or more of the following strategies:
(Check one or more)

___ used objects
___ drew a picture
___ made a chart
___ made an organized list
___ looked for a pattern
___ worked backwards
___ thought of a simpler problem
___ guessed and checked
___ used logical reasoning

___ E. Persisted until the problem was solved
___ F. Found the correct solution to the problem (48)
___ G. Checked the accuracy of the solution without prompting
___ H. Counted to determine the correct number of tiles
___ I. Added to determine the correct number of tiles
___ J. Multiplied to determine the correct number of tiles

Use assessment booklet pages 26–27 for questions 15 and 16.

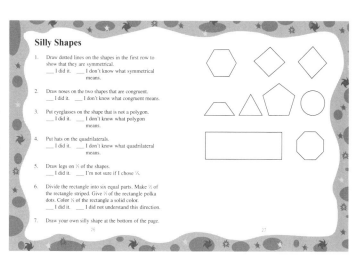

15. **Use pages 26 and 27 of the booklet.** *I'll say the names of shapes and you point to them.* Check the shapes that your child could identify:
    ___ hexagon (six sides)
    ___ octagon (eight sides)
    ___ pentagon (five sides)

16. *Follow the directions on this page to make silly shapes.* Check all that apply.
My child understood these terms:

___ A. symmetrical (equally balanced)
___ B. congruent (same size, same shape)
___ C. polygons (shape with three or more sides)
___ D. quadrilateral (shape with four sides)
___ E. one-third (three of the shapes should have legs)
___ F. 1/3, __, 1/6 (If your child divided the rectangle into six boxes, three should have stripes, two should have polka dots, and one should be a solid color. These boxes can overlap—stripe and polka dotted—leaving some boxes white.)

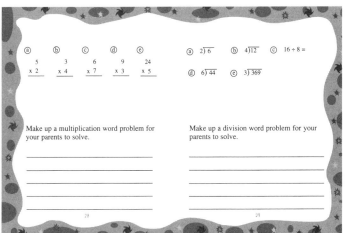

Use assessment booklet pages 28–29 for questions 17 to 20.

17. **Use page 28 of the booklet.** *Can you do these multiplication problems?*
Write a story problem.
Check all that apply.

___ Can solve problems a–d correctly
___ Can solve problem e correctly
___ Attempted the problems but made errors
___ Cannot do multiplication at this time

If your child could not do these multiplication problems, STOP. Go to question 21.

18. *Can you write a multiplication word problem for me to solve?* After your child has written a problem, try to solve it. Then check all that apply:

    ___ A. Did not want to attempt to write a problem
    ___ B. Began to write a problem but did not know how to incorporate multiplication as the task
    ___ C. Wrote a problem that calls for a function other than multiplication
    ___ D. Wrote a story but did not phrase it as a problem
    ___ E. Wrote a problem that does not contain enough information
    ___ F. Wrote a word problem (ending in a question) that can be solved by multiplying.

19. **Use page 29 of the booklet.** *Can you do these division problems?* Check all that apply.

    ___ Solved problems a and b correctly
    ___ Solved problem c correctly
    ___ Solved problem d correctly
    ___ Solved problem e correctly
    ___ Cannot do division at this time

20. *Can you write a division word problem for me to solve?* After your child has written a problem, try to solve it. Then check all that apply:

    ___ A. Did not want to attempt to write a problem
    ___ B. Began to write a problem but did not know how to incorporate division as the task
    ___ C. Wrote a problem that calls for a function other than division
    ___ D. Wrote a story, but did not phrase it as a problem
    ___ E. Wrote a problem that does not contain enough information
    ___ F. Wrote a word problem (ending in a question) that can be solved by dividing

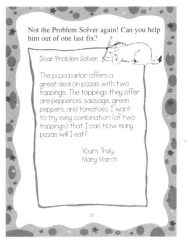

Not the Problem Solver again! Can you help him out of one last fix?

Dear Problem Solver,

The pizza parlor offers a great deal on pizzas with two toppings. The toppings they offer are pepperoni, sausage, green peppers, and tomatoes. I want to try evey combination (of two toppings) that I can. How many pizzas will I eat?

Yours Truly,
Mary March

Use assessment booklet page 30 for question 21.

21. **Use page 30 of the booklet.** *Can you solve this problem? Remember, show your work.*

Check all that apply.

____ A. Read and understood the problem

____ B. Came up with a plan for solving the problem

____ C. Expressed confidence (or seemed confident) while attempting to solve the problem

____ D. Used one or more of the following strategies:

(Check one or more)

____ used objects

____ drew a picture

____ made a chart

____ made an organized list

____ looked for a pattern

____ worked backwards

____ thought of a simpler problem

____ guessed and checked

____ used logical reasoning

____ E. Checked the accuracy of the solution without prompting

____ F. Found a correct solution to the problem

Assessment Guide

This guide will tell you what the data you've collected on the "Parent Observation Pages" means. It will also direct you to the activity sections in the book that are most appropriate for *your* third grader.

Reading Assessment

Question 1

This question will help you determine which strategies your child is using to decode words. If your child is relying on strategies that don't seem to be working, see "Reading Comprehension," page 64; "Word Study," page 87; and "Spelling," page 122. If your child struggled through most of this passage, you may also want to see "Reluctant or Struggling Readers," page 101. If your child could read this passage with ease, it's likely that he or she uses a number of successful approaches to reading.

Question 2

These questions help you to determine whether or not your child understands what he or she reads.

Question A asks your child to recall the events of the story in correct sequence.

Question B asks your child to recall a detail.

Question C asks a vocabulary question. If your child did not know this word prior to reading this passage, this question will help you to determine if your child uses context clues to figure out the meaning of new words.

Question D encourages your child to use critical thinking skills to evaluate the information in the text.

If your child could read the words but had difficulty answering any of these questions, see "Reading Comprehension," page 64. If your child particularly enjoyed answering question D, see "Reading and Writing Enrichment," page 130, for activities that support and extend your child's reading and writing.

Question 3

Good readers are constantly making predictions. They predict what a story will be about, what a character will do next, how the story will end. If your child was reluctant to make a prediction or if you think he or she could use more practice in this skill, see "Reading Comprehension," page 64.

Question 4

Again, these questions will help you to determine how well your third grader understands what he or she reads.

Question A asks that your child summarize the story.

Question B asks another vocabulary question. If your child had not heard the word "culprit," could he or she determine the meaning from the context of the story?

Question C encourages your child to draw a conclusion.

Question D encourages your child to compare and contrast.

Question E is another higher level thinking skill. Could your child respond?

Question F assesses your child's knowledge of compound words.

Question G assesses your child's familiarity with synonyms and his or her ability to identify them.

If your child had difficulty with any of questions A through E, see "Reading Comprehension," page 64. If your child had difficulty with questions F and G, see "Word Study," page 87. If your child enjoyed answering question E, you might want to try some of the activities in "Reading and Writing Enrichment," page 130.

Questions 5 and 6

Your third grader should have many experiences in word study and become increasingly familiar with the dictionary this year. Questions A through C test your child's knowledge of words. If he or she had difficulty with any of these questions, see "Word Study," page 87. Questions D through F ask your child to apply his or her knowledge of the dictionary. If your child had difficulty with any of these questions, see "Study Skills," page 96.

Question 7

These questions assess your child's comprehension and knowledge of nonfiction articles.

Questions A and B ask your child to identify the main idea and supporting details.

Question C asks your child to draw a conclusion based on information in the text.

Question D asks your child to identify the type of passage.

Question E will help you to determine what your child knows about research.

If your child had difficulty with questions A through D, see "Reading Comprehension," page 64. If your child had difficulty answering question E, see "Study Skills," page 96.

Question 8

This question surveys your child's reading habits. These are the habits exhibited by growing, enthusiastic readers. If you did not check at least four of these habits, you may want to see "Reading Comprehension," page 64. If you only checked one or two of these habits, you may also want to see "Reluctant or Struggling Readers," page 102.

Writing Assessment

Knowing where your child is in the process of learning to write will help you respond to written work and support his or her growth as a writer. If you have any concerns about questions A through E, or the survey your child completed, see "Writing as Communication," page 104, and "Spelling," page 122. If your child needs help in preparing oral presentations, see "Oral Presentations," page 127. If you have any concerns regarding questions F through K, see "Editing," page 117. If your child is not beginning to use cursive writing with some confidence, see "Cursive Writing," page 128. Remember, writing and reading skills naturally reinforce one another. Help your child to become a better writer, and you will help him or her to become a better reader as well.

Math Assessment

Question 1

To be truly successful in math, children must develop proficiency in problem solving. They must develop strategies to help them comprehend problems, seek solutions and identify reasonable answers. They need to learn that problem solving requires inquiry and persistence, but it can be genuinely fun, too.

- If you did not check A–F, see "Problem Solving and Logic," page 134, for ways to help your child grow as a problem solver.
- If you did not check G, see "Number Sense," page 140, in addition to "Problem Solving and Logic."
- If you did not check H, review the value of coins with your child. Skim "Number Sense," page 140, for ideas on how. (You might want to see "Working Below Grade Level in Math," page 179, if your child continues to have difficulty retaining the value of coins.)
- If you did not check I, see "Place Value with Addition and Subtraction," page 146, to give your child additional practice in adding two digit numbers.

Question 2

By third grade, your child should demonstrate an ability to work with numbers through the hundreds—estimating, adding, and subtracting. If your child could not estimate the sum or the difference (within twenty) on any of these questions, see "Number Sense," page 140. If your child made two or more errors while adding or subtracting, see "Place Value with Addition and Subtraction," page 146.

Question 3

Math students who understand the concept of place value have not simply memorized computation tricks ("carrying" or "borrowing"). They recognize that there is more than one way to work with numbers to arrive at the correct solution. This question assesses your child's understanding of place value and flexibility in working with larger numbers. If your child could not come up with a second way to add or subtract, see "Place Value with Addition and Subtraction," page 146.

Question 4

An understanding and recognition of patterns leads to a more thorough understanding of such math functions as multiplication and division. If your child could not complete these patterns, see "Number Sense," page 140.

Question 5

A genuine understanding of the relationship between addition and sub-traction, and being able to complete missing addend sentences, are skills third graders are ready to grasp. If your third grader could not complete these sentences in one minute, provide activities that will reinforce the connection between these functions. You may also want to help your child to memorize addition and subtraction facts. See "Number Sense," page 140, for ideas on how to do both.

Question 6

Measuring area and perimeter are new skills for many third graders. To help your child get a leg up in learning these concepts, see "Measurement," page 156.

Question 7

If your child needs help in recognizing capacity, see "Measurement," page 156.

Question 8

If your child could not give two or more correct responses to this question, try to determine why. Is your third grader familiar with liquid capacity (pints, quarts, half-gallons, gallons)? If not, see "Measurement," page 156. Can your third grader work with simple fractions (1/4, 1/8, _)? If not, see "Fractions," page 163.

Questions 9–13

This year, your child should be able to tell (and show) time to the minute. He or she should also be able to add and subtract time with the use of a clock, calculate elapsed time, and use a calendar. If your child had difficulty answering any of these questions, see "Measurement," page 156.

Question 14

This question gives you another chance to assess your child's problem-solving skills and will help you to determine which computation processes your third grader is most comfortable using. Watch to see if your child is developing a repertoire of strategies. Does he or she recognize that different types of problems require different tools to solve them? (Question 21 will give you additional help in evaluating your child's range of strategies.)

• If you did not check A through G, or if your child automatically used the same strategy to solve this problem as in question A, see "Problem Solving and Logic," page 134.

- If you did not check G, and your child came up with an improbable answer, you might also want to see "Number Sense," page 140.
- If you checked H, your child has chosen a process that will work, but he or she may need more work with faster functions, such as adding and multiplying. If so, see "Place Value with Addition and Subtraction," page 146, and "Multiplication," page 150.
- If you checked I, see "Multiplication," page 150, for activities to do next.
- If you checked J, or if your child solved the problem using quick logical reasoning, you may also want to see the activities in "Math Enrichment," page 184.

Question 15

Could your child identify these shapes? If not, see "Geometry," page 166, for activities that will help you to introduce them.

Question 16

A through D assess your child's understanding of geometric concepts. These are essential for later learning. If your child could use assistance in learning about these concepts, see "Geometry," page 166. E and F assess your child's knowledge of fractions. If your child had difficulty with either of these questions, see "Fractions," page 163.

Question 17

This is the year that your child learns his or her multiplication facts. If your child could not solve problems a–e correctly, see "Multiplication," page 150. If he or she could solve problems a–d correctly, but it took more than a minute, you might want to review the memorizing fact activities in "Number Sense," page 140, (in addition to activities in "Multiplication") to help your child solve problems like these more quickly.

Question 18

It's important for third graders to go beyond memorizing the "times table." They need to be able to apply their knowledge to problem solving. Writing a multiplication word problem asks your child to demonstrate his or her understanding of the concept of multiplication. If you checked A through C, see "Multiplication," page 150, for activity suggestions. If you checked D or E, it is likely that your child could use more practice in "Problem Solving and Logic," page 138. If you checked F, you may want to explore some of the activities in "Math Enrichment Exercises," page 184.

Question 19

Problems a and b determine if your child can do simple division facts. Problem c determines if your child recognizes the divide symbol. Problem d determines if your child knows how to record remainders, and question e determines if your child can divide with a three-digit dividend. To help your child with problems a–c, see "Introduction to Division," page 177. Children in the third grade are usually not expected to solve problems such as d, but if your child knew what to do, you might want to explore some of the activities in "Math Enrichment," page 184.

Question 20

This question assesses whether or not your child understands the concept of division. If not, see both "Multiplication," page 150, and "Introduction to Division," page 177. (The more work your child does with multiplication, the more prepared he or she will be for the concept of division.) Again, if your child had difficulty writing a word problem, see "Problem Solving and Logic," page 134, to provide more experience with problems.

Question 21

This question can provide you with one more look at your child's approach to problem solving. It can also help you to determine whether your third grader can apply his or her knowledge of division and fractions to problem solving.
- If you did not check A through F, see "Problem Solving and Logic," page 134, for further help.
- If you did not check F, see "Probability and Statistics," page 172.

Math curricula are not uniform around the country. It is likely that your child has been introduced to many of the concepts here, but has never heard of others. If your child struggled with this assessment, talk to her teacher. Find out how well this assessment matches what your child is actually being taught. Ask your child's teacher if your child is working on or below grade level. ("Working with Your Child's Teacher," page 188 and "Working Below Grade Level in Math," page 179 might help.) If your child had little or no difficulty with the assessment, skim the book for exercises that would interest you and your child most. Feel free to adapt them in any way that is appropriate. You may also want to explore the activities in "Math Enrichment," page 184.

Remember, this is the time to impart the knowledge that math—discovering patterns, playing with numbers, and solving problems like a sleuth—can be fun. Help your child to love math. Let that be your directive.

Reading Exercises

Reading Comprehension

The ability to comprehend what is read is measured by questions 1, 2, 3, 4, 7, and 8 on the Reading Assessment.

"I am so glad my son's reading has taken off. That's one concern we can put behind us."

This is a sentiment commonly expressed by the parents of third graders, who often feel, especially if their child had an easy time learning to read in first and second grade (or earlier), that third grade is a time to relax and pay less attention to reading development. On the contrary, your third grader has just begun to learn the skills he will need to become a lifelong reader. His future academic success rests on his ability to grow—to develop his skills in comprehension and to analyze the vast amounts of information with which he will be presented.

Reading is so much more than the ability to decode words, to read sentences aloud, or to answer questions. Reading is the ability to use the written word to grasp an underlying meaning, to extend one's understanding of the world, to question the truthfulness or validity of something, and to apply those words to one's life. It is the ability to live vicariously. One day a reader might find himself totally abandoned on a mountain in Maine, another day he is riding a cart on the underground railroad. On yet another day he laughs at an ingenious solution to a school problem or is inspired to stand up to the kid who won't stop bullying him. Reading arouses a child's imagination, allows him to sympathize with people of different ages and cultures, and helps him to know himself. Quite simply, it enlarges his world.

Many parents suddenly realize, when their children reach the junior high years (and often long before), that somewhere along the line, their children failed to learn to *love* to read. That their children would do almost anything before picking up a book. That reading assignments in school are always dreaded—or worse, skipped. And that a classic such as Shakespeare's *A Midsummer Night's Dream* or even Edith Wharton's *Ethan Frome* are as difficult to read as decoding words was back in the first grade. What happened?

Like learning to play the piano or speaking a new language, reading is a skill that must be practiced. Your child may enjoy books now, but unless you are diligent about promoting reading in your home, it is likely that he will become distracted. As children begin to participate in more activities outside the home, reading becomes the forgotten choice. (How many adults do you know who admit to never picking up a book?) If a child stops choosing to read, he will not get the practice he needs, and this will affect his future learning.

> ## BUILD A HOME LIBRARY
> You can find books at reasonable prices at yard sales, secondhand book stores (some bookstores have a section of secondhand books), and a children's book club. Begin a tradition of buying your child new books on special occasions. Some families have found the home library so valuable that they make a monthly trip to the bookstore. If this isn't in your budget, try making regular trips to your public library.

The good news is that there are four things you can do to ensure that your child continues to grow as a reader. These four things will also enrich your life, as well as the quality of time you spend with your child, immensely.

1. Read aloud to your child.
2. Encourage your child to read daily.
3. Help your child to read for specific purposes.
4. Help your child apply critical thinking skills to reading.

Read Aloud to Your Child

What is your fondest memory of school? Many adults, when asked this question, will tell about a time a teacher read to them. Not the kindergarten teacher, mind you, but a middle school or even a high school teacher! And not only do these adults remember the teacher, they remember the name of the book and the excruciating wait that occurred between suspenseful chapters.

You probably established a time to read aloud to your child when he was young. You offered your lap or some other cozy place to explore the wonder and excitement of books. By reading aloud, you taught your child how books work, how written language sounds, how thrilling stories can be. But did you know that your child needs to be read to now as much as he did when he was four?

There are many worthwhile reasons for reading to your third grader. First of all, your child can understand books that are at a higher reading level than the ones he can read independently. By choosing and reading books that are slightly more sophisticated than those he reads himself, you are introducing new vocabulary, new sentence structures, and more complex ideas. You are also whetting his appetite for the fascinating stories that are to come. By letting him know that one day *he* will be able to read all of the Redwall or the Narnia books on his own, you will be assuring him that reading is well worth the effort.

Second, by reading aloud, you are giving your child practice in picturing the story. In our visual age of television, videos, and computers, the ability to imagine gets less and less practice. And yet it is absolutely necessary for visualizing, and subsequently understanding, stories.

Third (and this is perhaps most important), by reading aloud you communicate how much *you* value reading and spending time with your child. As you read, you and your child share new worlds together. From time to time, you can take turns reading—by alternating books, chapters, or even paragraphs. In this case, you will be there to help your child develop new strategies, to help him make sense of new words or concepts. You will also be there to cheer him on.

One last note: Some parents are nervous about reading aloud—especially to older children. They worry that they'll stumble on some of the words, or that they'll read without expression. That's OK. Everyone, no matter how proficient, stumbles on words. When this happens, go back and correct yourself. In doing so, you give your child permission to take risks, to make mistakes, *and* you will show him how readers self-correct for meaning. You are presenting yourself as a learner. Modeling goes a long way in supporting your child's reading success.

MORE THAN ONE CHILD?

Try to find some evenings when you can read to each child separately. One-to-one attention has a profound effect on how children listen and respond to stories. They are more apt to concentrate, to ask questions, and to connect the story events and the emotions of the characters to their own lives when they are the only listeners.

HAVE FIVE MINUTES?

➤Read picture books to your child. Most third graders love to revisit the stories they read when younger, either because the problems presented are still relevant (*Where the Wild Things Are* is as likely to touch the heart of the sometimes powerless eight-year-old as it did the rambunctious four-year-old) or because they enjoy looking back at the stages they've grown beyond. In addition, many gorgeous and engaging picture books are being published for older children these days. Children's book publishers realize that the TV generation loves books with visual images, and no longer looks upon the picture book as babyish. Ask your local librarian to direct you to books for middle graders, or check out some of the books on the list at the right.

➤ Read a poem to your child. Invite him to tell you the picture the poem conjured up in his mind. If he has difficulty visualizing a scene, tell him what you imagined. Let him know, however, that the same words can create very different pictures to different people. You may enjoy sharing scenes that you picture while reading aloud, and talking about how they are the same and how they are different. (For a list of poetry books that third graders are sure to enjoy, see page 113.)

➤ Collect interesting articles, poems, or quotes to read aloud at dinner. One night you might share an article about a current movie. Another night you might read a poem about the value of making mistakes. Encourage everyone in the family to be on the lookout for bits to read. And enjoy the lively discussions that are bound to follow!

➤ Read the Sunday or daily comics aloud. It's much more fun to laugh together.

➤ Do Reader's Theater. You read the dialogue of one character; your child reads the dialogue of another. Try to make your voice match the personalities of the characters.

➤ Read everywhere: at breakfast, on the subway, right after school, or whenever you're waiting for another child's event to end. You might want to carry a paperback in your back pocket for those opportune times.

HAVE MORE TIME?

➤ Read to your child the books you loved as a child. Perhaps you remember reading *The House at Pooh Corner, The Secret Garden, Charlotte's Web,* or *The Wind in the Willows.* Your child will find these stories as relevant today as you did when

Picture Books for Third Graders

- *The Adventures of Sparrowboy,* by Brian Pinkney (Simon & Schuster)
- *Amelia's Notebook,* by Marissa Moss (Tricycle Press)
- *Chicken Sunday,* by Patricia Polacco (Philomel)
- *The Lotus Seed,* by Sherry Garland (Harcourt Brace)
- *Mississippi Mud: Three Prairie Journals,* by Ann Turner (HarperCollins)
- *My Life with the Wave,* by Catherine Cowan (Lothrop Lee & Shepard)
- *Potato: A Tale from the Great Depression,* by Kate Lied (National Geographic)
- *Painting the Wind,* by Michelle Dionetti (Little, Brown)
- *The Paper Dragon,* by Marguerite Davol (Atheneum)
- *Seven Brave Women,* by Betsy Hearne (Greenwillow)
- *Snapshots from the Wedding,* by Gary Soto (Putnam)
- *When Jessie Came Across the Sea,* by Amy Hest (Candlewick)

you were his age. Unfortunately, many children are exposed to these classics in their animated movie form long before they are ready to hear them read. Consequently, they become too familiar or, as in the case of Winnie the Pooh, are interpreted as being more appropriate for younger children. But no child enjoys the wit of A. A. Milne more than the eight- or nine-year-old. Consider this excerpt:

Read-Aloud Chapter Books

- *The Borrowers*, by Mary Norton (Harcourt Brace)
- *The Cricket in Times Square*, by George Selden (Yearling Books)
- *Clara and the Hoodoo Man*, by Elizabeth Partridge (Dutton)
- *Daughter of Suqua*, by Diane Johnston Hamm (Albert Whitman)
- *Frindle*, by Andrew Clements (Simon & Schuster)
- *Half Magic*, by Edward Eager (Harcourt Brace)
- *I Thought My Soul Would Rise and Fly: The Reconstruction Diary of Patsy*, by Joyce Hansen (Scholastic)
- *Lost on a Mountain in Maine*, by Donn Fendler (Beech Tree Books)
- *Maniac Magee* or *The Library Card*, by Jerry Spinelli (Little, Brown)
- *Pippi Longstocking*, by Astrid Lindgren (Viking)
- *Shiloh* and *Shiloh Season*, by Phyllis Reynolds Naylor (Bantam Doubleday Dell)
- *The Whipping Boy*, by Sid Fleischman (Morrow)

> "Oh!" said Pooh, and scrambled up as quickly as he could. "Did I fall on you Piglet?"
> "You fell on me," said Piglet, feeling himself all over.
> "I didn't mean to," said Pooh sorrowfully.
> "I didn't mean to be underneath," said Piglet sadly.

This delightful humor is entirely missed on the younger child.

➤ Respond to your child's questions with careful explanations. Consider this conversation between a parent and child:

> "Mom, what does stupor mean?"
> "Mmm. Let's see. A kind of confusion, I think. In this case the dragon is in a stupor because he just woke up."
> "Like Dad when he first wakes up in the morning?"
> "Yes. [Mom laughing] You could say your father is in a stupor until he's had his first cup of coffee."

By being patient and exploring the child's questions, you are broadening his knowledge base and vocabulary. Your child's proficiency at reading and understanding more challenging books will grow right along with this new information. This way, your child won't hesitate to ask when he doesn't understand a word, or if the events in the book don't make sense to him.

➤ Read classic (but lesser-known) fairy tales such as Shirley Climo's *The Egyptian Cinderella* (Crowell) or Margaret Hodges's *Saint George and the Dragon* (Little, Brown). Then read "fractured fairy tales"—spoofs on well-known tales or the tale told from a different point of view.

➤ Dramatize favorite scenes from stories you read aloud. Most third graders welcome a chance to don costumes and a new persona, especially when Mom or Dad get into the act. Encourage your child to use his own words when speaking rather than trying to remember the dialogue from the books.

Encourage Your Child to Read Daily

There may be controversy over which method is the best for teaching children to read. But everyone who has ever studied reading agrees on this simple and undeniable truth: The more a child reads, the better she becomes.

Reading improves your child's vocabulary. With practice, your third grader will gain speed and a greater understanding of what she reads. And the more satisfied she is with reading, the more likely she will continue to read, and the more she will grow into an independent, competent reader.

Without realizing it, parents can get in the way of their child developing a strong reading habit. When days get busy, reading time is often forgotten. Extracurricular activities, homework, socializing, computer, and TV time take its place. But research shows that when children stop reading, they begin to fall behind their classmates. Their test scores in vocabulary, comprehension, and advanced thinking skills go down. So do their writing scores. And worst of all, they forget the value and pleasure of reading a good book. So do your part by scheduling regular reading time, limiting TV and computer play, and creating an atmosphere in which everyone loves to read. The following activities may help you.

HAVE FIVE MINUTES?

➤ Give your child access to books. Most schools send home flyers from popular book clubs. These books are sold at terrific discounts. (And for every dollar you spend, your child's teacher receives points toward books for the classroom.) Help your third grader frequent the local library. You may want to include a stop at the library as part of your regular trips to the grocery store or Laundromat.

➤ Let your child read series books. You may have enjoyed reading the Hardy Boys, the Bobsey Twins, or the Nancy Drew books when you were a child. Well, they're all still around, as well as other prolific series, such as the Baby-sitters Club, the Boxcar Children, and Goosebumps. These books have familiar characters that face familiar problems in familiar ways. By picking up the next book in the series, your child skips that awkward stage of learning about the

Folk and Fairy Tales

- *The Hired Hand: An African American Folktale,* by Robert D. San Souci (Dial)
- *The Little Seven-Colored Horse: A Spanish American Folktale,* by Robert D. San Souci (Chronicle)
- *Rapunzel,* by Paul O Zelinsky (Dutton)
- *Rikki-Tikki-Tavi,* by Rudyard Kipling, adapted by Jerry Pinkney (Morrow)
- *The Girl Who Lived with the Bears,* by Barbara Diamond Golden (Harcourt Brace)
- *Androcles and the Lion,* retold by Dennis Nolan (Harcourt Brace)

Fractured Fairy Tales

- *Goldilocks and the Three Blairs,* by Marilyn Tolhurst (Orchard)
- *Prince Cinders* and *Smarty Pants,* by Babbette Cole (Putnam)
- *Rumplestiltskin's Daughter,* by Diane Stanley (Morrow)
- *The Three Little Pigs and the Big Bad Wolf,* by Eugene Trivizas (Scholastic)
- *The True Story of the Three Little Pigs* and *The Stinky Cheese Man and Other Fairly Stupid Tales,* by John Scieszka (Viking)

setting and characters and puzzling out the author's style. Don't be concerned if your child insists on reading only these books for a while. She is getting much needed practice, and most children will move on to more stimulating books in time. In fact, many parents find that the series are often springboards for other literature.

Short Chapter Books

- *The Blue Hill Meadows*, by Cynthia Rylant (Harcourt Brace)
- *Drew and the Bub Daddy Showdown*, by Robb Armstrong (Harpercrest)
- *Flat Stanley*, by Jeff Brown (HarperCollins)
- *Freckle Juice*, by Judy Blume (Scholastic)
- *The Good, the Bad, and the Goofy; The Not-So-Jolly Roger;* and others, by Jon Scieszka (Viking)
- *How Can I Be a Detective If I Have to Baby-Sit?* and other mysteries by Linda Baily (Albert Whitman)
- *A Mouse Called Wolf* and *Ace, the Very Important Pig*, by Dick King-Smith (Knopf)
- *Mr. Fantastic Fox* and *George's Marvelous Medicine,* by Roald Dahl (Puffin)
- *My Name Is María Isabel,* by Alma Flor Ada (Atheneum)
- *Pirates Promise,* by Clyde Bulla (HarperTrophy)
- *Rent a Third Grader,* by B. B. Hiller (Scholastic)
- *Sadako and the Thousand Paper Cranes,* by Eleanor Coerr (Bantam)
- *The Secret of the Seal,* by Deborah Davis (Random House)
- *Spider Storch's Teacher Torture* and others, by Gina Willner-Pardo (Albert Whitman)
- *T.J.'s Secret Pitch,* by Fred Bowen (Peachtree)
- *Tales of the Wicked Witch* and others, by Hanna Kraan (Front Street)

➤ Show your child how to choose a book that she'll enjoy. Many third graders do not read regularly because they have difficulty finding good books. The next time you're at the public library, suggest she search for a cover or a title that piques her interest. Next, suggest she turn to the middle of the book (around page thirty) and read a page or two. (The first pages of a book are often slow or full of description. Authors try to hook readers instantly, but they often do it better once they get going.) Ask her to count the number of times she comes to a word she doesn't know. If she finds more than five unknown words on a page, that book is probably too hard for her to read on her own. (You might want to check the book out for reading aloud, though.)

If your child still wishes to bring home picture books, don't discourage her. Reading is reading. Many picture books are actually written at a higher reading level than beginning chapter books. If, however, you feel she constantly chooses books that are below her reading level, entice her with more challenging books when you read to her. Stop reading at an exciting point. It's likely that she won't wait for you to finish the book!

What if your child chooses books that are too hard? Most middle grade readers do this from time to time. Suddenly it seems as if the whole world of reading is open to them—even books for adults—and they want to flex their newfound reading muscles. Again, support your child's attempts. Either she will be so motivated to get the information that she struggles her way through (it's amazing what kids pick up when they're driven in this way) or she will realize that she's happier reading books at her own level.

On the opposite page is a list of chapter books that are short and easy to read, and on this page, below, is a list of middle grade novels that your child is bound to enjoy.

➤ If you've brought books home from the library, but your child still isn't reading them, read the information on the front flap of the jacket cover, or on the back of a paperback, aloud. Often this will launch her into the book. Or read the first few chapters and let your third grader take over from there. Check back with her every now and then to see how she's coming along.

➤ Don't overlook the biography section of the library. Third grade teachers report that most eight- and nine-year-olds enjoy a good biography, and some will read every biography they can get their hands on! See the list of biographies on the following page.

➤ Give your child some background information on the book she's reading. If she has chosen *Number the Stars* by Lois Lowry, tell her a little about the Nazi occupation during World War II. If she has decided to read the picture book *Jackie Robinson: He Was the First* by David A. Adler, you might talk a moment about race discrimination and the color barrier. Don't worry if you don't know what the topic of her book is, or if you don't have the necessary background information. Sometimes it helps just to be near while she's reading and to help her with a word or a concept she has never heard before.

➤ Let your child see you reading a book simply for pleasure. Research has shown that children who read have parents who read.

➤ Show interest in what your child is reading. Ask her what the story is about in the same way you would ask a friend about a book. Now and then pay her the ultimate compliment, and ask, "May I read that book when you're through?" (If you do read the book, find a time when the two of you can talk about your favorite parts.)

Middle Grade Novels

- *Addie's Forever Friend,* by Laurie Lawlor (Albert Whitman)
- *The Cat Who Went to Heaven,* by Elizabeth Coatsworth (Simon & Schuster)
- *The Classroom at the End of the Hall,* by Douglas Evans (Front Street)
- *Coco Grimes,* by Mary Stolz (HarperCollins)
- *Walking the Starlight Bridge,* by Alice Mead (Farrar)
- *Muggie Maggie* and *Ramona Quimby, Age 8,* by Beverly Cleary (Morrow)
- *Mean Margaret,* by Tor Seidler (HarperCollins)
- *Red Dirt Jesse,* by Anna Myers (Walker)
- *Stone Fox,* by John Reynolds Gardiner (HarperCollins)
- *Sun and Spoon,* by Kevin Henkes (Greenwillow)

➤ Scatter a variety of reading material around your house. Let your child read books, magazines, comics, travel brochures, poetry—whatever catches her fancy. Don't hide books on the top shelves or newspapers in baskets. Leave them around and open where they can catch an unsuspecting eye. You may want to give your child a subscription to a magazine. If you're not sure which one to subscribe to, check them out at a newsstand or your library. Here is a list of some exceptional children's magazines for the third grader.

- *American Girl* 800-234-1278
- *Boy's Life* 972-580-2352
- *Cricket* 800-827-0227
- *Highlights* 888-876-3809
- *National Geographic World* 800-437-5521
- *Sports Illustrated for Kids* 800-992-0196

HAVE MORE TIME?

➤ Talk about stories or facts learned in nonfiction books. Mother/daughter book clubs are cropping up all across the country, and they provide wonderful opportunities for girls to read books that involve strong female protagonists. Experts suggest that one reason why boys stop reading at a young age is that they don't talk about books among themselves the way girls do. So perhaps it's time to focus on our sons and their need to talk about good books, too.

Biographies

- *Alice Ramsey's Grand Adventure,* by Don Brown (Houghton Mifflin)
- *A Boy Called Slow: The True Story of Sitting Bull,* by Joseph Bruchac (Philomel)
- *Alvin Ailey,* by Andrea Davis Pinkney (Hyperion)
- *Coming Home: From the Life of Langston Hughes,* by Floyd Cooper (Philomel)
- *Eleanor,* by Barbara Cooney (Viking)
- *Finding Providence: The Story of Roger Williams,* by Avi (Harpercrest)
- *Frederick Douglas: The Last Day of Slavery,* by William Miller (Lee & Low Books)
- *George Washington: A Picture Book Biography,* by James Cross Giblin (Scholastic)
- *Gertrude Chandler Warner and the Boxcar Children,* by Mary Ellen Ellsworth (Albert Whitman)
- *How My Family Lives in America,* by Susan Kirklin (Simon & Schuster)
- *Keep the Lights Burning, Abbie,* by Peter Roop (Carolrhoda)
- *Minty: A Story of Young Harriet Tubman,* by Alan Schroeder (Dial)
- *Walter Dean Myers,* by Diane Patrick Wexler (Raintree/Steck Vaughn)

Help Your Child to Read for Specific Purposes

Reading fulfills many purposes. We read for pleasure, to visit new places, live other lives vicariously, to solve a good mystery, to laugh out loud. We read for information, to answer questions, to find solutions, to make sense of the world. And we read to communicate, to feel a greater connection to others, especially those with whom we have things in common.

Third graders, with their curious and social nature, and their desire to expand their horizons, begin to seek information from many different sources. They realize now that books are written for different purposes, and upon arrival at the library will run for the encyclopedias, the section on fairy tales, or the *Guinness Book of World Records,* depending on their interests.

Help your child to pursue his interests and learn about school subjects by suggesting appropriate books and identifying new sources of written information.

HAVE FIVE MINUTES?

➤ Support your child's inclinations by giving him access to the books he loves. Does your child like to read mysteries? Comic books? Scary stories? Help him get his hands on his favorite genre. Nothing hooks a person like reading for fun. Stop everything and read that juicy novel you've been saving too.

➤ Read joke and riddle books to reinforce the knowledge that reading is pleasurable. Whereas the younger child enjoys riddles for the sheer delight of asking a question and getting a silly answer, third graders now have the sophistication to understand wordplays and puns. Look for books that will make your child laugh—and you groan—over and over again.

➤ Look for amazing fact books that are sure to entertain your third grader. One such book is *Weird but True* by Janet Goldenberg. Of course, the most commonly known amazing fact book is the *Guinness Book of World Records.* Many teachers have launched the reluctant reader by placing this book in his hands.

➤ Help your child to identify different literary genres. Your third grader should become familiar with the terms "fiction," "nonfiction," "reference," and "folktales." Show your child how libraries are arranged according to these labels. You might even suggest that your child arrange his own books using these categories.

➤ Ask your local librarian to recommend books that speak to your child's particular concerns. Fiction often presents themes such as adoption, divorce, the ups and downs of friendship, the many configurations of families, having special needs (or living with a sibling with special needs), prejudice, sibling rivalry, and more. There are also nonfiction books on these topics. A powerful shift occurs when children realize that life's problems can be shared through books.

► **Finding Answers** As third graders become more competent readers, they gain confidence and interest in using reference books. Have people always slept on pillows? Do walruses have hair? Who *was* Cleopatra, anyway? Third graders no longer need to badger partially attentive adults with questions, they can turn to books for answers! You can support this growing skill by answering questions with the question, Where could we find that out?

Help your child to realize that there are a number of places to find answers. Most people automatically think of the encyclopedia, and this is a great place for third graders to begin. If you are not within walking distance of your local or school library, you'll probably want to own some type of encyclopedia. You might want to purchase a used set from a yard sale, the want ads, or your local library. (An incomplete set is even better than no set, although you'll swear that you always need the letter you don't have!) If you have a computer, you can buy an encyclopedia on **CD-ROM** or gain access through the Internet. There are even paperback desk encyclopedias that sell for around eight dollars. These are more like dictionaries than comprehensive encyclopedias, and they lack the illustrations that tend to hook children, but they will answer questions in a pinch.

Other reference books to look for are dictionaries, almanacs, atlases, and nonfiction books on topics your child has a strong interest in. It is likely that your child will have to write some kind of report this year, and he may get to choose the topic. If he's a castle aficionado, having access to David McCauley's book *Castles* will certainly help him in finding information. (For a list of nonfiction books, see right.)

Whether your child has regular access to a library or has reference sources at home, show him how to use these books in an efficient manner. You can find activities for helping your child to gain knowledge about reference books in "Study Skills," page 96.

> ## WHAT IS A RELUCTANT READER?
>
> The term "reluctant reader" is applied to the child who is struggling to learn to read. If your third grader avoids reading for any reason, he or she needs your help. See page 101 for suggestions.

HAVE MORE TIME?

► Help your child follow a set of directions to cook a dish, make a craft, or enter a contest. There are many "how to" books for children at your local library. Search for a project you can do together.

➤ If your child has a particular interest—model cars, natural disasters, soccer, rocks, historical dolls—help her to pursue them. Read information in books, magazines, and on the Internet. Write letters to experts or stars. Suggest your third grader keep a scrapbook of all the facts, interesting articles, or letters he's collected.

Help Your Child Apply Critical Thinking Skills to Reading

As mentioned, learning to read is much more than recognizing words on a page. Consider this passage from Janet Taylor Lisle's award-winning book *Afternoon of the Elves:*

"You just wouldn't, none of you!" [Sara-Kate] shrieked, losing control in a way most unlike her. She began to run and hop along the hall in the strangest fashion, with knotted fists and flying feet. Like an elf, Hillary thought.

In order to understand these three sentences, the reader must be able to use the following critical thinking skills:

- identify events in sequence (What do you think happened before Sara-Kate yelled?)
- determine cause and effect relationships (*Why* did Sara-Kate yell? What caused this loss of control?)
- draw conclusions (Why, do you think, the comment angered Sara-Kate?)
- compare and contrast (How does Sara-Kate usually act? How is she acting differently now? Why does she remind Hillary of an elf?)
- use context clues (What does "knotted fists" and "flying feet" mean?)
- make predictions (What will happen next?)
- summarize (What was this story about?)

These skills are best sharpened not by answering questions in a reading skills workbook but by interacting with others. At school, your child can develop these skills by talking with other readers or the teacher in literature discussion groups. At home, your child can learn these skills

Nonfiction

- *Anthony Reynoso: Born to Rope,* by Martha Cooper (Clarion)
- *A Drop of Water: A Book of Science and Wonder,* by Walter Wick (Scholastic)
- *Baseball in the Barrios,* by Henry Horenstein (Gulliver)
- *Baseball Just for Kids: Skills, Strategies and Stories to Make You a Better Ballplayer,* by Jerry Kasoff (Grand Slam Press)
- *The Children's Atlas of Lost Treasures,* by Struan Reid (Millbrook)
- *Day of the Dead,* by Tony Johnston (Harcourt Brace)
- *Disaster! Catastrophes That Shook the World,* by Richard Bonson and Richard Platt (Dorling Kindersley)
- *Elephant Woman: Cynthia Moss Explores the World of Elephants,* by Laurence Pringle (Simon & Schuster)
- *Get on Board: The Story of the Underground Railroad,* by Jim Haskins (Scholastic)
- *Kente Colors,* by Deborah M. Newton Chocolate (Walker)
- *Orcas Around Me: My Alaskan Summer,* by Leslie W. Bowman (Albert Whitman)
- *Outside and Inside Bats,* by Sandra Markle (Atheneum)
- *Watching Water Birds,* by Jim Arnosky (National Geographic)

simply by talking with you. Here are some ways to address each of the specific skills.

Identify events in sequence

The story events in books for young readers are usually written in a simple, chronological order. Books for middle grade children and older, however, start to play with time. Some stories begin in the middle of a scene of action, or a conversation, and then revert back to the beginning. Others are told with any number of flashbacks. Mysteries often give a series of clues that make sense only when the sequence of events are puzzled out.

Let your child know that authors do not always present necessary information immediately. The first few paragraphs of a chapter book may begin with only a hint of what the book is about. Instead of opening with the setting and a description of the characters (for example, Once upon a time in the land of Nod, there was a small boy), the book may begin with dialogue or a vague description. Consider the first sentences in *Finding Walter* by Ann Turner:

> The trouble was the mice. And the moths. Sometimes the spiders. They had taken over the dollhouse that lay in the attic, out of sight, forgotten since Alice had grown up and gone away.

"Huh, I don't get this. What's this story about?" you may hear your third grader, who likes stories to move in a straight line, exclaim. Advise her to read on. Tell her that the information she needs, the questions she wants answered, will come.

If you fear that your child will pass up a good book simply because of the opening sentences, then you read the first few pages aloud and pass it off to her.

To help your child with sequencing, and comprehending differences in style, try some of these activities.

HAVE FIVE MINUTES?

➤ Read aloud the first chapter of a book to your third grader. Then hand the book over to be read independently. The next day, ask your child to catch you up on what's happened in the story. If she leaves out important events, ask for clarification.

➤ Ask your child about her day. As mentioned in the "Developmental Overview," she may begin by telling you every detail of every moment, or she may be so overwhelmed by details that she answers with a quick "nothing." Don't be put off (as hard as that is) by either reaction. Ask specific questions:

> *What are you studying in science?*
>
> *When did the astronomer come to your class?*
>
> *What will you do first to prepare for the science fair?*
>
> *You made a mobile? How did you do it?*

By regularly sharing the news of her day, your child will practice important skills such as sequencing and summarizing. You may even find her storing tidbits and anecdotes in her memory that she knows you will enjoy.

➤ Encourage your child to make a comic strip of the important events that took place in a favorite book. Many children love illustrating the stories that have touched their hearts.

➤ Or cut up a comic strip and challenge your child to put it together again in the order that makes sense.

HAVE MORE TIME?

➤ Photocopy the "What a Morning!" activity on page 215. Ask your child to cut the strips apart and place them in the correct sequence. Suggest she pay close attention to words such as "before" and "after" as well as a logical progression of activities. If she places them in the correct order, your third grader will be able to create a word using the first letter from each strip.

➤ If your child is required to do a book report, suggest she complete a graphic organizer *as* she reads the story. (A graphic organizer is a chart, a visual way to sort information.) She might want to use the Time Line or the Story Map found on pages 216–217 of this book (make multiple copies) or she may want to use a technique she has learned in school. Completing a graphic organizer while reading will help her to read with purpose, provide practice in sequencing, build her comprehension, and give her an outline to follow when preparing for her presentation.

Determine cause and effect relationships

Story plots are built on the understanding of cause and effect. Why did Robin Hood steal from the rich? To give the money to the poor. Why did Charlotte spin words into a web? To save her friend's life. Why did Mary Poppins leave? She knew that the Banks family no longer needed her. Help your child to think about cause and effect, and you will help her to understand the deeper meaning of books.

HAVE FIVE MINUTES?

➤ Raise cause and effect questions as you drive or walk to your destinations: What do you suppose caused those bushes to bend that way? Why is this shop closed today? What might have caused that accident? Likewise, support your third grader's incessant curiosity by answering her questions. Help her to explore possible causes when she raises "why" questions.

➤ While waiting in line at the grocery store, post office, or movies, play the But So game. Begin by stating a desired action, followed by "but," such as "I wanted to make a cake, *but* I didn't have any eggs." Your child follows this with a "so" statement. Alternate in a silly conversation that goes something like this:

> I wanted to make a cake, but I didn't have any eggs.
> So I went to a chickencoop.
> But the hens wouldn't lay.
> So I went to the grocery store.
> But the eggs were sold out.
> So I went to my neighbor to borrow an egg.

When you lose interest in one strand, reverse roles. Your third grader will love this nonsense game—though others waiting may just give you their place in line!

➤ Take turns cutting pictures out of magazines and placing them on the refrigerator. Invite other family members to look at the picture during the day and decide what happened just *before* the picture was taken. Then, at dinner, ask everyone to share his or her ideas. You'll be surprised at the range of creative responses! After you have tried this activity for several nights, suggest that everyone guess what happened *after* the "picture of the day" was taken.

> ➤ Help your child and his siblings or friends perform a play. Have them reenact a favorite story or write a play themselves. Creating and performing in dramatic productions helps children recognize the cause-and-effect links between story events. If you have access to a video camera, you might help your child record and edit scenes.

Draw conclusions

One of the major developmental differences between a beginning reader and a more advanced reader is the student's ability to make inferences or to draw conclusions. (Student textbooks often separate these two skills, but the differences between them are so slight that even teachers get them confused.) Consider this passage from Judy Blume's *Blubber:*

> **A loud noise came out of Linda then. At first I wasn't sure what it was but then the smell hit me and I knew. I wondered if she'd had sauerkraut for breakfast because that's what happens whenever Kenny eats it.**

Without its being explicitly stated in the text, you know exactly what has happened to Linda. To determine this, you combined your own experience and knowledge with the information that was given in the text to draw a conclusion. This is a skill that good readers develop.

HAVE FIVE MINUTES?

> ➤ The next time you and your third grader are at the mall or another public place, look at the people around you and draw conclusions about them. Ask: Where do you think that person is going? What do you think that person wants to buy? Why? Get your child to articulate the reasons for his conclusions.

> ➤ When you talk to your child about her day, ask her why she thinks certain things did or will occur: Why do you think Mr. Smith changed the day of the spelling test? Why do you think Tamara said that to you? How do you think you will do at the track meet?

> ➤ **Character Sketch** Ask your child to make a list of the personality traits the main character exhibits. For instance, after reading about how Ency-

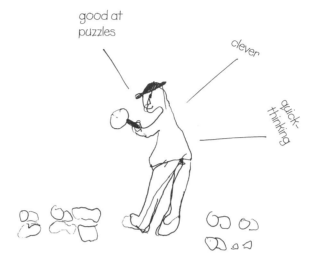

clopedia Brown solves a case, your third grader might draw the conclusion that this character is clever, quick-thinking, and good at puzzles. She may enjoy drawing a picture of the character and writing the traits on "pull outs."

good at
puzzles

clever

quick-
thinking

HAVE MORE TIME?

➤ Play chess with your child. Playing chess (and possibly other games that require strategy) actually increases a child's reading ability. Each time you make a move in chess, you take in information, draw upon experience, and draw conclusions.

If you and your child have never played chess together, play the first few games by revealing your strategies (call them practice games). Talk out loud while you move the chess pieces. For instance, you might say, "I see that you just moved your bishop in line with my knight. I suspect you are going to capture this piece, so I will move it here and at the same time get closer to your king."

➤ While reading a novel aloud to your child, stop periodically and ask such questions as: Why do you think he said that? Why do you think she made that choice? If your child says, "I don't know," don't respond immediately. Quietly wait for a few moments. Some children simply require more time to put their thoughts together. These children get used to adults not waiting, so they stop trying. If you discover that your child requires additional time to respond confidently, communicate this observation to your child's teacher. Your feedback will help the teacher to build more "wait time" into her lessons.

Compare and contrast

How are the characters alike? How does the setting of this book differ from the setting of others we've read? What is the difference between realistic fiction and fantasy? What other books does this book remind you of? All of these comprehension questions require the third grader to compare and contrast. If you frequently hear your child say, "His piece is bigger than mine," or "You always listen to his side first," you may think your child already has a good handle on this skill. But being able to compare elements of literature requires a more sophisticated form of abstract thinking than comparing two slices of chocolate cake. Working with your child as she develops the skill of comparing and contrasting is as much fun as hearing a toddler put two words together to make a sentence. You will be amazed at the insightful connections she draws.

HAVE FIVE MINUTES?

➤ After reading a picture book with your child, begin a conversation with "That book reminds me of (another book) because . . ." Encourage your child to look for and share her own comparisons.

➤ **Character Chart** Draw a quick, three-column chart for your child. At the top of each column write the headings "Things the Character Did," "I Have Done This," "I Have Not Done This." Invite your third grader to complete the chart by recording four or more actions in the first column. Then have her check the column that applies to her.

Things the character did	I have done this	I Have not Done this
Stevie crawled into a Dumpster		✓
She spied on people	✓	
She went outside on a rainy night	✓	
She caught the thief		✓

If completing a chart that is not required homework seems outlandish to your third grader, add a fourth column with the heading: "I Bet My Parent(s) Have Done This." Have your child guess whether you have done certain things in the past that she would like to know about!

➤ Draw a Venn Diagram like the one shown below. In one circle, ask your child to write all of the traits that describe the storybook character. In the other circle, have her write traits that describe herself. In the space where the two circles intersect, have her write those traits that describe both the character and herself. Your third grader may want to see if her teacher would approve of such a diagram for one of her book report requirements.

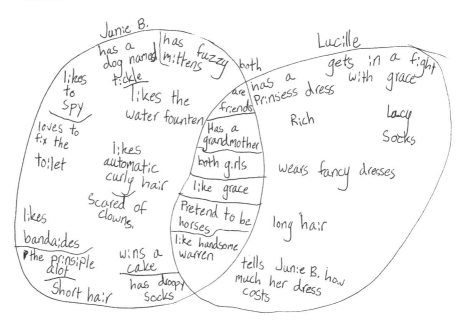

Based on the Junie B. Jones Series by Barbara Park (Random House).

➤ Have your child make a Venn Diagram to compare the setting in the book with a real setting. For instance, after reading the Laura Ingalls Wilder *Little House* books, have your third grader compare her home or school to Laura's. Or have your child compare the settings of two different stories.

HAVE MORE TIME?

➤ Have a friendly debate. Invite the family (and friends, too) to watch a movie together. Then make two signs. On one write the word "Agree;" on the other, write the word "Disagree." Startle everyone by taping the signs up in opposite corners of the room. Next, make a fairly controversial statement, comparing the movie you just watched to another familiar movie or television show. For instance, you might say, "The *Wizard of Oz* is a much scarier movie than *Star Wars.*" Have family members stand under the sign that represents their point of view. (If all members go to one sign, you go to the other.) Then invite each side to state their reasons. Go back and forth as long as the discussion remains fun for everyone.

Use context clues

"The presentation was so long and so boring, I vowed that I'd never glumut to attending another again."

What do you do when you're reading and you come to a word you don't know? You probably make a very good guess based on what comes before and what comes after the word. Without the use of a dictionary, you likely assumed that *glumut,* the invented word above, meant "to agree to" or "to give in."

Using context clues is a powerful tool. Every time your child comes across a new word and puzzles out the meaning, she is adding a word to her vocabulary. As her vocabulary grows, she's able to read increasingly difficult books, which, in turn, help her to learn the meaning of more new words. Reinforce this cycle with the following activities.

HAVE FIVE MINUTES?

➤ **Background Knowledge** Read the cover flap or the back of a new book. Then help your child make connections between her life and the lives she is going to read about. "Amber Brown gets the chicken pox? Remember what you went through when you got those itchy spots?" Encourage your child to talk about her experience. The more connections she makes, the more she will be able to use the context to determine the meaning of new words or expressions.

➤ If your child asks what a word means, use it in several sentences. Then ask her to tell you what she thinks the word means. For instance, if the word she asks about is "subtle," you could say, "The principal didn't come out and tell us to behave, she was more *subtle* than that." Or, "My friend wasn't being *subtle* when she said that my breath smelled bad."

> ## TIPS FOR USING CONTEXT CLUES
>
> - Model the strategy of going back and reading a sentence or two over whenever you have difficulty with a word or a passage. Let your child know that this is not only acceptable, it is a strategy all good readers use. Encourage your child to reread whenever necessary.
> - If your child stalls when she comes to a new word, have her skip it and go on. Then encourage her to go back and try to guess what the word says.
> - Help your child get into the habit of asking "What would make sense here?" when she comes to an unknown word.

➤ The next time you're at a restaurant, and the take-out menu has stories or descriptions, cross out every sixth word. Using context clues, ask your child to figure out what words have been deleted. Compare her answers with another menu. You can also use a children's magazine or catalog descriptions.

HAVE MORE TIME?

➤ Read aloud Lewis Carroll's nonsense poem "Jabberwocky" from *Through the Looking Glass*. It's a rollicking poem that describes a wondrous battle, but many of the words were invented by Carroll. Here is the first line:

> Twas brillig, and the slithy toves
> Did gyre and gimble in the wabe.

Suggest that your child tell you what she imagined after hearing the poem in its entirety, or better yet, ask her to draw a picture. Then discuss how she was able to understand the poem when none of the words were real. Help her to see that the position of words in a sentence gives clues to their meaning. "Jabberwocky" may even inspire your child to write her own nonsense poem.

Make predictions

Making and then confirming or revising predictions helps readers to stay fully engaged in a story and to read more fluently. As readers develop this skill, they predict what words say and mean, how characters will behave, and how the story problem will be solved. In other words, they constantly check their own understanding of the story.

HAVE FIVE MINUTES?

➤ Before reading, have your child study the cover and the illustrations in the book. Ask, What do you think this book will be about? When do you think the story took place? Who do you think the main character will be?

➤ If your child is reading nonfiction, suggest she preview what's to come. Have her read chapter titles, headings, captions to photographs, and charts ahead of time. Ask, What do you think you will learn?

➤ As you read aloud, stop and invite your child to predict how the story will end. Read on a little bit and then ask, Do you want to change your prediction? When you get to the end ask, Was your prediction correct?

➤ Play Who Am I? To make good predictions, your child needs to search for clues. Choose the identity of a book character, celebrity, or neighbor with whom your child is familiar. Give your child clues such as "I lived with my two brothers until my mother asked us to make our own way in the world. I needed a new home, so I decided to build one" (one of the three little pigs). Then switch roles.

Summarize

The ability to summarize is a skill that will be taught throughout your child's school career. Why? Because learning to condense a story, a movie, or an article into just a few sentences is hard work. If you think about it, you probably have a friend or relative who still runs up your phone bill because of an inability to be concise!

Learning to summarize will help your third grader to write more cohesively. Here are some ways to get your child started.

HAVE FIVE MINUTES?

➤ Help your child understand that magazine and newspaper articles, reports, and nonfiction essays (such as an encyclopedia entry) have a main idea. Read a brief and interesting newspaper article to your child and have her tell you the single, most important fact she learned.

➤ Challenge your child to tell you the main idea of an article or personal narrative in a single breath. This will help reinforce the knowledge that the main idea is a phrase or a sentence (or two).

➤ Write a thank-you note. Suggest that your child think about a main idea and details as she writes. For instance, the main idea may be: "I love the soccer ball you gave me." Details would be: "My friends and I taught ourselves to play soccer. We play every Saturday. I'm the only kid in the neighborhood with a ball, so everyone depends on me to bring mine. Next year, I'll probably sign up to play soccer at school."

➤ Being "brief" can be tough for the ardent third grader. When your child is required to summarize a story for school, suggest that she write it as a telegram. Give her an index card to write her telegram, or challenge her to write it within a given number of lines.

➤ Idea Umbrella: Later, when your child has become accustomed to thinking about a main idea, tell her that the main idea is supported by several details. Again, read a brief magazine or newspaper article that would interest her. Then draw an umbrella. Together, write the main idea of the article at the top of the umbrella. Write the supporting details on the frame lines.

When your third grader writes a personal narrative or a report, have her prewrite by thinking about the main idea and supporting details first.

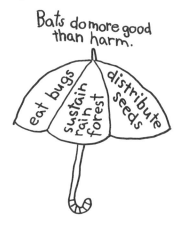

She might want to draw an umbrella as a way to organize her thoughts.

➤ When your child attempts to summarize a fictional work, suggest that she remember CAPS.

C = characters

A = action the characters take (or what the characters want)

P = the problem that occurs

S = the solution that solves the problem

So, a summary of *Charlotte's Web* could be stated this way: "It's about a pig named Wilbur and a spider named Charlotte who become friends. Wilbur is going to be slaughtered. But Charlotte writes special words about Wilbur in a web and saves his life."

To give your child additional practice in organizing her thoughts, have her complete a Story Map (see page 217).

➤ Whenever you read an interesting article or story, tell your family and friends about it. Include a brief summary. Hearing you summarize will help your child organize her thoughts into a cohesive summary.

Remember: Learning to summarize takes lots of practice. If you can help your child organize her thoughts after reading, she will begin to recognize key elements for summarizing *while* she reads.

Word Study

The ability to recognize the meaning of and analyze words is measured by questions 1, 4, 5, and 6 on the Reading Assessment.

As children grow as readers, they begin to recognize that words are built with predictable spelling patterns (specific phonics and decoding strategies are described in "Spelling," page 122). They learn that words can be broken apart and reconfigured according to syllables and base words. They discover that words can have multiple meanings, similar meanings, and opposite meanings. They also discover that some words sound alike but are spelled differently and have very different meanings.

You may remember word study as drudgery. But believe it or not, there are people who love words. There are those who love the way words roll off the tongue, the images they create, and how they can change your mood. Then there are those who view words as historical puzzles. They love discovering the origin of a word, how the meaning of a particular word has changed, or what popular culture is doing to that word. There are others who spend half of every Sunday completing the crossword puzzle in a newspaper, or beating friends and family at Scrabble. And then there are some who take great pride in being word police. They know the proper way to use and spell words and they are sticklers for correctness. The one thing these people have in common, though, is they have discovered the joy that comes from learning about words. And this is something you and your child can do, too.

Try to create a spirit of exploration in your child. Instead of just handing him an English workbook, invite your third grader to join you in marveling at words.

There are at least five areas of word study, in addition to phonetic spelling, that your child will be exposed to this year:

vocabulary development
syllabication
synonyms and antonyms
homonyms
compound words
word structure (verb endings, prefixes, and suffixes)

Vocabulary Development

The growth and development of a student's vocabulary plays a large part in his ability to progress as a reader. In homes where conversation, questions, and reading are encouraged, children hear and apply new words with relative ease. Here are a few more ways to build your child's vocabulary.

HAVE FIVE MINUTES?

➤ Read to your child—books, magazines, poetry, newspaper articles, recipe cards, it doesn't matter. This is one of the most successful ways to introduce new words. If you haven't already, see the read aloud activities and book recommendations in "Reading Comprehension," page 64.

➤ Have thoughtful conversations with your third grader. In many homes, most language directed at children consists of instructions: Take out the trash. Do your homework. Pack your snack. Although necessary, these instructions do not give children practice in hearing and using precise words. Build a time into your routine, perhaps over morning toast or right before bed, when you can discuss why the moon waxes and wanes or why some baseball teams are named after birds.

➤ Post a word of the day. Use the word in a number of sentences until your third grader can guess its meaning. For instance, if the word of the day is "improvise," you might say, "I didn't have an envelope, so I had to improvise and use part of a paper bag." Or "You improvised a toy chest from some old wooden crates." Let your child show you that he "gets" what the word means by using it in his own sentence.

It probably won't be long before your third grader asks if *he* can post the word of the day. By all means, encourage him to do so. As this activity becomes part of your normal routine, your new wordsmith will begin to collect stumpers of his own.

➤ Next time you're waiting at the dentist's office with your child, play Which Word? Write several words that your child is likely to have heard but is not yet including in his everyday speech, on a sheet of paper. For instance, you might write "reservations," "instigated," "fiddled," and "observant" on a sheet of paper. Then choose one word and give your child clues until he guesses the word you are describing. Clues might be definitions (this word means that someone is good at seeing things) or sentences with a blank (You saw that cardinal in the tree. You are so *blank*.)

HAVE MORE TIME?

➤ Play word games to expose your child to new words. Here are a few old favorites: Spill and Spell, Boggle, Scrabble for Juniors, Pictionary Junior. Your child will practice building words on his turn, you will get the chance to introduce your child to new words on yours.

➤Attend concerts, plays, and cultural events. Go to museums and exhibits. Talk about what you see and hear.

Syllabication

Your child probably has had some experience in dividing words into syllables. Being able to divide words into parts helps a reader figure out long words (particularly when they have been broken up at the end of lines) and a writer to build new ones. As your child learns the rules for syllabication, he will begin to make better spelling choices.

HAVE FIVE MINUTES?

➤**Word Clap** Check to see if your child recognizes segments by asking him to clap on the syllables of a long word. Say "windsurfer." Does he clap it out this way: wind/sur/fer? Say refrigerator. Does he recognize all five syllables? If not, practice clapping out syllables together. Have your child go on a syllable hunt to find words with one to five syllables.

> IDENTIFYING LONG WORDS
> When you are reading aloud to your child or any time you come across an unfamiliar name or long word ("predominate," for example), model breaking the word into syllables to figure it out. Put your finger over all but the first syllable and read that syllable (pre). Then move your fingers so that only the first two syllables show and blend the two syllables together (pre/dom). Continue until you've sounded out the entire word.

➤To give your child practice in dividing words into syllables, make up imaginary, multisyllabic words such as "frogboffer" or "mustallow." Have your child tell you what the words say by first dividing them into syllables and then reading them back to you.

➤Teach your child this simple rule of syllabication for two-syllable words: When a short vowel (*a* as in cat, *e* as in net, *i* as in sit) is followed by two consonants, the word is divided between the consonants (flip/per, stop/ping). When the word has a long vowel, the word is divided after the vowel (mu/sic, pa/per). Knowing this rule will help your child with spelling. Imagine this conversation:

> Mom, does buzzer have one z or two?
> Is the vowel long or short?
> Short. Oh! There must be two z's.

HAVE MORE TIME?

➤ Teach your child how to write haiku, traditional Japanese poetry that follows this specific three-line structure:

five syllables
seven syllables
five syllables

Contemporary poet Alison Herschberg, abandoning the classical nature themes, writes:

Hard Crunchy Pretzels
What did you say? I can't hear—
My teeth are breaking.

And a third grader, inspired while scraping the dinner dishes, wrote:

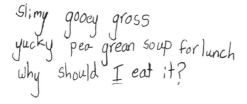

Slimy gooey gross
yucky pea grean soup for lunch
why should I eat it?

Synonyms and Antonyms

Synonyms are words that are *almost* the same in meaning. "Yell," "shriek," "holler," and "shout" are synonyms. However, synonyms are not always interchangeable. "'Dinner,' Mom hollered" connotes a different meaning than "'Dinner,' Mom shrieked." The goal, when introducing synonyms to your child, is to help him understand that similar words have different shades of meaning (What is the difference between holler and shriek?) and that authors try to choose the most precise word whenever possible. The greater your child's vocabulary grows, the more accurate his reading comprehension, writing, and speaking will become.

Teachers often have a list of what they call marshmallow words. These are words we use in everyday speech that have become too soft and rather meaningless. "Nice" is a marshmallow word third graders use often: Our new car is nice. My Aunt Helen is nice. Having a picnic in the winter was nice. Help your child to recognize marshmallow words and choose more exact words instead:

Our new car is roomy. My Aunt Helen is sweet. Having a picnic in the winter was exciting (and a little cold). Other marshmallow words are walk (try: saunter, march, hike, stomp, meander, pace, step, tiptoe), bad (try: rotten, mischievous, wrong, evil, inappropriate, poor, shabby), and words that have become too familiar in everyday speech, such as cool or awesome.

Antonyms are words that are nearly opposite in meaning. Hard and soft are antonyms. So are hard and gentle. Here are some activities to help your child focus on the many shades of word meanings.

HAVE FIVE MINUTES?

➤ Buy your child a thesaurus, a book of synonyms intended to help writers choose more precise words. To the lament of many a creative writing teacher, children who are just beginning to use a thesaurus arbitrarily substitute too many words with those that are long and pretentious—after all, long must be better, right? Wrong. Nevertheless, if you and your child's teacher can put up with a period of thesaurus overuse, you will have found a way to introduce your child to new vocabulary and the concept that words can be exact. Two beginning thesauruses that are easy for the third grader to use are *The American Heritage Children's Thesaurus* by Paul Hellweg (Houghton Mifflin) and *A First Thesaurus* by Harriet Wittels and Joan Greisman (Golden Books).

➤ Make a word search. Instead of just searching for words, have him write antonyms as clues. Let's see, the clue is "confusing," should I look for "clear" or perhaps "understandable"? Have your child time you to see just how long it takes for a grown-up to work his puzzle out! (Tip: Creating word searches using graph paper, or even lined paper, is easier for the eight-year-old than working on blank paper.)

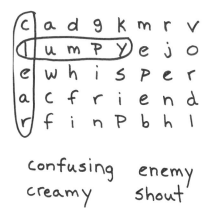

➤ Play My Uncle Joe. Begin by choosing an adjective to describe fictitious Joe. For instance: "My Uncle Joe is mean." Have your third grader and other family members emphasize what you have said with synonyms: "He's low! He's despicable! He's monstrous! He's dastardly! He's nasty! He's hateful!" Then let other players begin a round with a new adjective. When your child has become familiar with this game, suggest that he contradict you with antonyms: "Uncle Joe is kind! He's generous! He's good-natured!"

➤ Have your child write synonyms for colors. For instance, synonyms for red might be crimson, ruby, scarlet, and cherry. How many can she come up with for the color green? Pink? Don't be surprised if your ingenious third grader goes running to a crayon box!

Homonyms

Homonyms (or homophones) are words that sound alike but are spelled differently and have different meanings. "There," "their," and "they're" are homonyms. So are "son" and "sun," or "blue" and "blew." The most frequent writing mistakes in both students' and adult writing are the use of incorrect homonyms. Now is the time to help your child create hooks for homonyms in that incredible memory of his.

Picture Books That Help

- *Eight Ate: A Feast of Homonym Riddles* and *Hey hay! A Wagonful of Funny Homonym Riddles,* by Marven Terban (Clarion)
- *A Chocolate Moose for Dinner* and *The King Who Rained,* by Fred Gwynne (Aladdin)

HAVE FIVE MINUTES?

➤ Want to surprise an unsuspecting third grader? Invite him to sit at the table or kitchen counter, whip out a can of shaving cream, and squirt a generous blob in front of him. Ask him to spread the cream around to make a good drawing surface. Then, using the homonym list on page 201, write a single word in the shaving cream. Challenge your child to illustrate the word correctly. (Some children like a goal to work for. If your child is one of these, tell him you will squirt out one "snowball" for every word he illustrates correctly. Stack the snowballs three high to make snowmen. How many snowmen can your child create?)

➤Play Homonym Pictionary. Take turns choosing a homonym pair from the list on page 201 and drawing pictures that represent both of the words in the order they are written. The player who guesses the illustrated homonyms gets a point. The player who correctly matches the pictures with the word spellings gets two points.

➤Write coded messages that include homonyms. Writing or deciphering a code helps children pay closer attention to individual letters. Challenge your child to solve the mystery message below using the pigpen decoder. Encourage your child to write his own homonym messages in code.

➤ Together, create a crossword puzzle using homonym pairs. Suggest your third grader write sentences with blanks for word clues—for example: "1 across. The wind _____ my hat away." If you have access to a photocopier, make copies of the puzzle so your child can challenge his classmates or Great-aunt Lucy.

Compound Words

Compound words are words that have been created by combining two words to make one. "Sunshine," "chalkboard," and "earring" are compound words.

HAVE FIVE MINUTES?

➤ Challenge your child to come up with as many compound words as possible that contain the word "sun." Here are a few: sunshine, sunbathe, Sunday, suntan, sunfish, sunlight. Other good words to begin with are "some" and "day."

➤ Next time you're waiting for the food to arrive at a restaurant, have your child search the menu for compound words. Can he find any of these: pancakes, cheeseburger, hotdog, milkshake, breadsticks?

➤ Still have time? Invite your third grader to write his own menu using compound words *he* invents. Caramelnoodles or coldpizza anyone?

HAVE MORE TIME?

➤ Ask your third grader if he has ever seen butter fly or a fish bowl. He may look at you funny for a moment until a brand-new, hilarious image replaces his old knowledge of these compound words. Suggest he draw comical pictures to illustrate other compound words. He may even want to bring a few favorites to school and have classmates guess the words he has illustrated. Here are some fun words to start with:

cowboy	cupcake	pigtail	playground
housefly	wishbone	carpool	laptop

Word Structure

Oh, if words would only stay the same! We take verbs and add endings: stop, stops, stopping. We combine words to make new ones: stoplight, stopwatch. And we add prefixes and suffixes: unstoppable. "Word study," or "structural analysis," examines the parts of a word and helps children recognize patterns. Here are a few activities to help your child feel a sense of command over constantly changing words.

HAVE FIVE MINUTES?

➤ Teach your child these two rules when adding the endings *-ing, y, er,* or *ed.*
  - *When a word ends in* e, *drop the* e *and add the ending.* (Examples: have-having, flake-flaky, trade-trader, hope-hoped)
  - *When a word has a single vowel, followed by a single consonant, double the consonant and add the ending.* (Examples: run-running, sun-sunny, flip-flipper, hop-hopped)

➤ If your child is having difficulty adding a particular word ending, such as *ing* or *er,* choose a discarded children's magazine and have him highlight words in the text with that ending. (Third graders are willing to do almost anything with a yellow highlighter!) Then have him tell you the spelling rule demonstrated.

➤ Next time you're passing time in the car, give your child words with endings and challenge him to tell you the base word. Let him know that in order to look words up in a dictionary, it's necessary to know the base word.

➤ Build words. Start with the word "friend." Take turns adding prefixes and suffixes to the word to create new words: friendly, friendship, befriend, unfriendly. Talk about how each word part changes the meaning of the word.

HAVE MORE TIME?

➤ Play Pantomimes with the suffixes *-ful* and *-ly.* Write the following words on cards: care, friend, loud, wild, cheer, play, slow, quiet, hope, pain. Take turns (1) drawing a card, (2) adding one of the endings (silently) to the word to a make a new word, and (3) acting out the new word. Can you guess what word is being pantomimed?

➤ The next time you play Scrabble, show your child how to increase his points by adding the prefixes *re-* (which means "again") and *un-* (which means "not") to words already on the board. Your third grader will be thrilled to turn "clog" into "unclog" and "play" into "replay." You may want to offer an extra five points if he can tell you what the new word means.

Study Skills

The ability to use study skills is measured by questions 5, 6, and 7 on the Reading Assessment.

Educators often say that in kindergarten, first, and second grade, children learn to read. In third grade and beyond, children read to learn. And although this is not entirely accurate (children continue to learn *how* to read long after third grade), there is a new emphasis in the middle grades on reading to obtain and apply information.

You can teach your third grader how to find information and develop good study habits by helping her to:

Use the library effectively

Learn dictionary skills

Recognize and use different parts of books

Gather and organize facts

Use the Library Effectively

Put most frankly, from now until your child graduates from high school, and well beyond, you want the library to be her second home. Imagine giving your child another place of comfort. A place where she can be surrounded by old friends (books, patrons, and librarians) where there are adults who know her interests and can guide her, even help her to learn, whenever they get the chance. Your public library offers all of this and more.

Make library visits an important part of your normal routine. Help your child get the lay of the land and give her the skills to enter those library doors confidently.

HAVE FIVE MINUTES?

➤ Teach one new skill each time you visit the library. By introducing one of the following concepts or tools before heading off to find the new releases, you will be helping your child become increasingly independent:

- Discuss the difference between fiction and nonfiction. Help your child find the fiction and nonfiction areas in your library. Point out that fiction is shelved according to the first letter of the author's last name. Nonfiction is shelved according to the Dewey decimal system. Walk up and down the aisles discovering how nonfiction subjects are shelved. What books do you find in the 500s? What about the 700s? The 800s?

- Show your child how to use the computer and/or card catalog. Demonstrate how to look up books by author, title, or subject.

Choose one of your child's passions. Cooking? Yoyos? Endangered
species? Find a list of books and where they are shelved.

- Together, learn the librarians' names. Librarians are your child's very
  best resource for information.
- Show your child the reference section and the types of books she will
  find there. Gradually demonstrate how to use encyclopedias,
  almanacs, and atlases. Perhaps there are books in the reference section that you didn't know existed. Your enthusiasm over an unknown
  resource will surely be catchy.

HAVE MORE TIME?

➤ Most public libraries offer a summer reading program for children. See if
this program doesn't hook your third grader.

Learn Dictionary Skills

Third graders are expected to learn basic dictionary skills and to practice
them so that those three little words "look it up" no longer instill panic or
resentment. Here are some ways that you can help your child find that one single word in a book of thousands.

HAVE FIVE MINUTES?

➤ Buy a child's dictionary for your third grader. Children's dictionaries
have fewer words, simpler definitions, more attractive illustrations and
larger type, all making the task of learning how to use a dictionary far
easier.

➤ Show your child how to alphabetize words to the third letter. Say, "Look
at the first letter. Which letter comes first in the alphabet?" If more than
one word has the same beginning letter, have your child move to the second or third letter. For instance, the following words would be alphabet-
ized in this manner: baffle, bag, bail. (Which word would come first,
"main" or "mainstay"? The word that runs out of letters!)

  Suggest that she make a list of things in one of her collections (bean
bag animals, baseball cards, gum wrappers) using alphabetical order.

➤ Demonstrate the use of the guide words at the top of the dictionary
pages. Point out that your phone book, as well as the dictionary, uses
guide words for faster word finding. Invite your third grader to find the
names of three of her friends in the phone book and tell you which guide
words the friends' names are under. If your child likes a good competitive
game, suggest you time how fast she can find a name in the phonebook or

a word in the dictionary. She's sure to discover that using guide words cuts many seconds off her time.

➤ Say a word and use it in a sentence. Then have your child look the word up in the dictionary and give you the *number* of the correct meaning. Some good words to start with are: star, tip, state, bother, guard. This activity will help your child recognize that words can have several definitions.

➤ Many computer programs now offer a dictionary, encyclopedia, and thesaurus, raising the question: Do children really need to learn how to use these books? To answer this question, race your child. You look a word up in the encyclopedia while she finds it on the computer. Which method of finding the information is faster?

HAVE MORE TIME?

➤ Introduce your child to the pronunciation key. Have her practice reading unknown words using the phonetic spelling. Then, write her a note using the phonetic spellings (as given in the dictionary) of many of the longer words. Challenge her to replace your words with the correct dictionary spellings.

> Dear Dora,
> Wut wŭd ū līk tü dü tə dā?
> luv,
> Mom

➤ Play Fictionary. This game requires three or more players and an adult dictionary.

FICTIONARY

1. One player chooses an unknown word from the dictionary.
2. Other players write a mock definition, trying to sound as close to the dictionary as possible. The player who chooses the word then copies the real definition (just one meaning) and reads that definition and the responses of the other players all in the same tone of voice.
3. Everyone tries to guess which definition is the correct one. Players get a point for choosing the correct definition. The player who selected the word gets a point each time someone chooses a wrong definition.

Recognize and Use Different Parts of Books

You pick up a book titled *Natural Disasters* and wonder if it has information on forest fires. What do you do? You might skim the table of contents, or you might turn directly to the index at the back of the book. Within moments you know whether this book has the information you're looking for. By helping your third grader learn these same skills, you will be saving her a good deal of time and frustration when looking for specific information.

HAVE FIVE MINUTES?

➤ Choose a collection of stories or a nonfiction book and show your child the table of contents. To demonstrate how much information can be found in these front pages, ask your child to be a detective and answer the following questions.

How many stories (articles) are in the book?
What is the name of the first story (article)?
On what page does (choose a selection) begin?
Which story (article) comes right after (choose a selection)?
Which story (article) begins on page (___)?

➤ Indexes can be found at the back of most nonfiction books. Find a book with an index, turn to the back, and ask your third grader to *tell you* what she notices about the index. She will probably come to the conclusion that subjects are listed alphabetically and are followed by page numbers. Ask, How would you use an index? When would you use an index?

➤ Graphic aids (charts, graphs, maps, diagrams) can also be a tremendous help in locating information and learning more about a topic. Point out graphics whenever you read a nonfiction book together. Show your third grader graphics when you come across them in the newspaper. Ask her to tell you how to read the graphic and what she has learned by it. (For more help in reading specific types of graphs see Probability and Statistics, page 172.)

➤ Show your child how to read a map. Draw her attention to the map key (legend) and scale. Practice measuring the distance between two points.

HAVE MORE TIME?

➤ To reinforce the advantages of graphics, have your child make her own chart. Ask her to consider which type of chart would be most useful. Here are some ideas that might be helpful:

- Make a chart of the things you need to do to get ready for school or ready for bed
- Make a chart that shows how you spend your allowance each week
- Make a chart of the things you *really* want to do in your spare time
- Make a chart that shows your favorite books, movies, or TV shows
- Make a chart that shows each family member's favorite foods

Gather and Organize Facts

Although your child has probably had a little experience in doing research, third grade is typically the year when children are taught to write their first report or are asked to research topics for homework. Here are some ways you can help your child gather the information she needs. (For more information on report writing, see "Writing as Communication," page 104.)

HAVE FIVE MINUTES?

➤ To help your third grader make sense of what she reads, demonstrate the use of a KWL chart. Fold a sheet of paper in thirds. Ask your child to label the paper with these headings: "What I *Know*," "What I *Want* to Know," "What I *Learned*." (Once she uses this strategy enough to remember the headings, she can simply use the letters *K*, *W*, and *L*.)

K — What I Know	W — What I want to know	L — What I Learned
That animals nead lift to fly and also air Pressure.	How long can insects fly? How do animals learn to fly? How do they get enough energy to fly long distensis? What is the fastest animal or insect?	That they get energy by eating rich foods. Pigeons can fly for hundreds of miles at more than 50 miles per hour. Birds fly higher and faster then any other animal. In some parts of the world there is flying frogs, snakes, lizards, squirrels an fish! I also learn different parts of what the feathers called!

Chart based on The Secrets of Animal Flight, *by Nic Bishop (Houghton Mifflin).*

Before she reads a book, advise her to record what she already knows about the subject in the first column. Then have her record what she wants to know in the second. Tell her that it's fine to add to this column as she reads. After she has read the book or article, have her record what she has learned.

➤ Before your third grader reads a book, have her look at photographs and read their captions, read chapter and section headings, and study any of the graphic aids. Encourage her to set a purpose for reading the material. For instance, your child might read a book on Pluto to determine its distance from the sun.

➤ Read a newspaper article to yourself (one that might interest your child as well) and highlight the most important facts. Then read the article to your third grader. Use your voice to give special emphasis to the highlighted information. Then ask your child to tell you the most important facts.

Although you are giving your child clues (the tone of your voice), she will eventually begin to read with the expectation that some facts are more important than others.

HAVE MORE TIME?

➤ **Organize Information** After your child has recorded notes from books, suggest she use different colored markers to underline or highlight the notes according to an organizational plan. For instance, if she has recorded facts about polar bears, she might underline facts pertaining to their habitat in green, facts pertaining to their diet in red, and facts pertaining to their behavior in yellow.

Reluctant or Struggling Readers

Children who are below grade level in reading are often referred to as "reluctant readers" by educators. By the third grade, children who have not begun to read with considerable fluency may appear to be reluctant. They probably groan when assigned reading skill work or research that requires reading. They likely avoid reading aloud or answering comprehension questions in class. No doubt they choose the thinnest books with the fewest number of words per page and, yes, will even fake reading.

But reluctant? Hardly. No one would choose the plight of the poor-performing reader. Struggling to decode words, to make sense of multisyllabic words, to create meaning from print is hard and often embarrassing work.

Children who are stumbling, reading word by painful word in the second half of third grade, desperately need your assistance. First of all, they need you to be their advocate. If your child has not been identified as a child who needs additional reading support and/or special school services, talk to his teacher. Suggest that your child be tested for any problems, such as a learning disability, which may be getting in the way of his reading.

Second, you must create a safe and supportive reading environment at home. Research has consistently proven that poor readers need two things: one-to-one support and lots of time spent reading as opposed to playing word games or completing skill workbooks. You are in the best position to provide both of these requirements. Tell your child that you will help him to grow into a capable and confident reader. Here are some ways to begin.

- Establish a time when you and your child can read together each day. Do not use this time as punishment ("Until you get your grades up, we're going to sit here and read") or take it away as reward ("If you clean your room today, you can skip reading time"). Practice reading in the same nurturing and supportive way you might help your child learn to make a grilled cheese sandwich or catch a baseball. Approach each session in a positive, you-can-do-it way.
- Take turns reading a book aloud. When it is your third grader's turn, try not to make him feel as if he's being tested. If he stumbles over a word, you might say, "I often stumble over words like that, too." If he comes to a word he doesn't know you can say, "What would make sense here?" or "What sounds do you see?" and then encourage him to keep going. Simply provide some words now and then to help your child keep momentum.
- Find books your child can read successfully *and* meet his interests. Help him to find stories about kids he can relate to. Your librarian will be your best resource. Remember that home is the place your child can practice reading without comparing page length, print size, or oral fluency with classmates. Don't let him label books as "baby books." Encourage him to read anything that catches his fancy and will help him feel successful.
- Until your child is reading beginning chapter books, sit down with more than one book at a time. If your child experiences success with one book, he'll probably want to start another immediately. Don't lose this perfect opportunity.

- Make reading a social event in your home. If you pressure your child to read, but everyone else is watching TV, talking on the telephone, or playing games, he'll feel isolated. Read with and beside your child. Share interesting facts or fun lines. Sigh when you get to the good parts.
- Talk to your child. Let him know that you recognize his efforts and that you have begun to search for ways to help him.
- Children in the third grade often find themselves reading more than one book at a time. They may read one book during formal reading time, another during independent reading time, and yet a third at home. This can be defeating for the emergent reader who is just learning to follow a story or stay involved in chapter books. If this is the case, ask the teacher if your child can stick to one book until completion. Suggest that he carry the book back and forth from school.
- Watch a movie with your child and then suggest he read the same story in book form. The movie will provide him with knowledge of the setting, characters, and plot—a tremendous boost for the struggling reader.

For Additional Support and Ideas

See some of the books listed below. Your library may have resources other than those listed here.

- *Solving Your Child's Reading Problems,* by Ricki Linksman (Citadel Press)
- *Unicorns Are Real,* by Barbara Meister Vitale (Warner)
- *Unlocking Your Child's Learning Potential,* by Cheri Fuller (Pinon)
- *Keys to Parenting a Child with a Learning Disability,* by Barry E. McNamara and Francine J. McNamara (Barrons)
- *Parenting a Child with a Learning Disability: A Practical, Empathetic Guide,* by Cheryl Gerson Tuttle and Penny Paquette (Lowell House)
- *Taming the Dragons: Real Help for School Problems,* by Susan Setley (Starfish)

Writing Exercises

Writing as Communication

Some say the art of writing is dead. But, in truth, this new age of communication has created the need for people of all walks of life to have skill in writing. Memos, e-mail, proposals, grant applications, and reports are standard fare in the workplace. On-line magazines and newspapers, chatrooms, and message centers create new forums for writing. The printed word is as alive and as creative as ever.

Most school curriculums include daily writing. Children at the third grade level write letters, reports, stories, responses to books they are reading, science observations, and explanations of how they solved a particular math problem. Teachers recognize that writing is not just an application of rules but a tool for thinking, a way to communicate, and a form of creative expression.

But teachers alone cannot give your child all the support he needs to develop into a strong writer. Some of the most important elements (modeling, appreciation, encouragement, time) best come from home. Here are ways that you can help your child to become a confident, skillful writer.

Model Writing

Gently point out the times when you have a writing task before you. "I think I'll make a list of things I have to do by the end of the week." "Wasn't it nice of Mrs. Murray to drop this rhubarb off? I think I'll write her a note." "I can't stand what's happening to our town park. I'm going to write a letter to the editor of the newspaper." "I've got to get into work early tomorrow—I have a big report to write." Whenever possible, share your writing. "Can anyone else think of something for my list?" "Do you think this letter will convince people to do something about the park?"

Do you feel like a broken record, asking your third grader to do the same thing over and over again? Instead, help your child focus (one of the developmental challenges of this age) by writing a note! Children respond well to a note. You won't have to nag and you've modeled writing!

Allow Your Child to Feel Ownership of His Writing

Many times a writer will share a piece of writing only to have everyone in the room tell him how to change it. "You should have the detective wear flippers instead of boots." "You should make the villain a frog." No matter how good the suggestions are, the writer is left feeling as if the story no longer belongs to *him*. And worse, he comes to believe that everyone else can do it better.

Whether he is completing a homework assignment, writing a postcard to Gram, or beginning his first science fiction story, let your third grader know that "he is the boss of his writing." All writers, even young ones, need to be motivated by their *own* ideas. They need to develop a confidence that tells them, *I* can do this!

Does this mean that you should butt out altogether? No! You can nudge your child into new growth by asking questions: "What made you decide to make the villain a cat?" "What exciting news are you telling Gram?" Or you can share your response to the work in an informative (not corrective) manner: "I loved the fact that the detective jumped into the water. But I wondered, How could he swim so fast with his boots on?" Your gentle feedback is likely to prompt your third grader to make changes, but changes he recognizes as his own.

Be a Supportive Audience

Good writing is always done with a purpose and an audience in mind. Children write to document, to inform, to respond, and most often, to entertain. Be positive in a way that meets your child's purpose. If your child is writing a story about elves that live in his closet, respond by telling him what parts intrigued you, made you laugh and wonder what would happen next. If he's writing every fact he knows about a major league baseball player, tell him which fact you found most amazing. If he writes to you just to say you're the greatest, let him know how powerful his words are.

What if parts are missing from the story, or several lines just don't make sense? Point out the parts that *are* working and then question your child. "Where did the elves come from? Why did they decide to move into your closet?" Asking a question or two will often send your child back to include a few more details. If he doesn't seem inclined to revise, say, "If you were going to include that information, where would you put it?" Even if your third grader doesn't want to change his story, he will begin to anticipate, while writing, the questions a reader is likely to have about his current piece and include more information. (For more revision suggestions, see "Revision," page 119.)

If you look at your child's writing, and the spelling and grammatical errors are the first and only things that jump out at you, refrain from commenting immediately. Discipline yourself to respond to your child's efforts to think and imagine first. Then, *after* you have responded as a good audience, feel free to point out *one* or *two* errors that your child is consistently making. If you point out more, your child won't be able to retain all that you're telling him and will become overwhelmed with the conventions of writing. You will not end up teaching him, only helping him to feel less capable. (Again, for more tips on correcting errors, see "Editing," on page 117.)

Writers Need Solid Chunks of Time for Writing

Good writing involves several stages that the writer cycles through over and over again. The writing process includes prewriting (generating ideas, choosing one, rolling the idea around for awhile, collecting facts, thinking), writing a first draft, reshaping, and revising it by adding or subtracting information, reordering ideas, choosing stronger words, and then editing—that is, cleaning up the punctuation and spelling. Don't underestimate the time it takes to write a thoughtful work. Know that whenever your child has been given a homework assignment that requires writing, he needs extra time to think and plan.

In first and second grade, your child was probably encouraged to write, write, write, without too much attention being given to form. In third grade, however, your child will learn that writing can be shaped to fit a particular purpose. In addition to supporting your child in the ways mentioned above, you can help your child learn about these specific writing forms:

letters
personal essays
stories
poetry
reports

Letters

This is the year that children usually focus on the form of the "friendly letter" (as opposed to a business letter). There are five parts to a friendly letter: heading, greeting, body, closing, and signature.

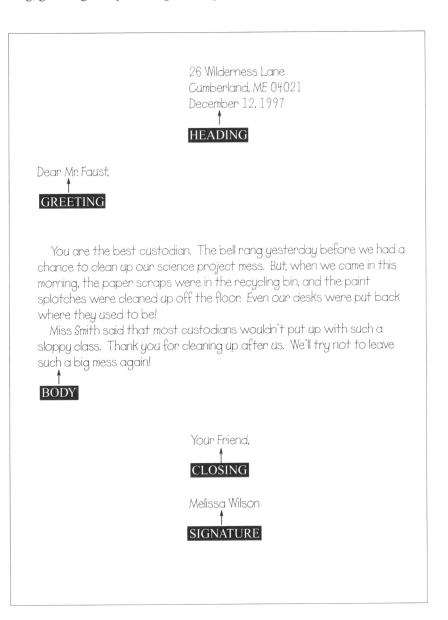

➤ Letter writing can be very gratifying since the effort is usually reinforced with a reply! Help your child make this connection by suggesting that he write a letter to

- a favorite TV, movie, or singing star
- a favorite author
- the manufacturer of a favorite toy or food
- the president of the United States
- a pen pal
- classmates who have moved
- relatives or seniors who are homebound

➤ Buy the book *Free Stuff for Kids,* published by Meadowbook. This book offers hundreds of places kids can write to receive "safe, fun, and informative things kids like."

➤ When your child needs a note to be excused from school for a dentist appointment or to explain an absence, have him write it. Then add your signature to his at the end.

HAVE MORE TIME?

➤ Take the time to read your local newspaper's letters to the editor together. You might find one on a topic that interests your child. In addition, most children's magazines have a page or two devoted to letters. Encourage your child to write a letter to an editor. Let him know that a well-thought-out letter has a good chance of getting published. (For a list of children's magazines, see page 73.)

Belles Lettres

There are some wonderfully clever books that tell a story, or impart knowledge, with the use of letters. Receiving one of these books is like receiving a whole mailbox full of lovely, personal mail. (And nothing is so juicy as reading someone else's letters!) Help your child to see proper letter form over and over again with these books:

- *The Gardener,* by Sarah Stewart (Farrar Straus Giroux)
- *The Jolly Postman,* by Janet and Allan Ahlberg (Little, Brown)
- *Letters from Felix; Felix Travels Back in Time; Felix Explores Planet Earth,* by Annette Langen and Constanza Droop (Abbeville Press)
- *Love Letters,* by Arnold Adoff (Scholastic)
- *The Magic Cornfield,* by Nancy Willard (Harcourt Brace)

Personal Essays

When people write about things from their own experience, they are more likely to show a greater depth of knowledge and perception and a greater commitment to writing. What they write will not only contain observations and details that are memorable, but they will ring true because they were there or because they gave a lot of attention to the subject. Writing about oneself and/or one's opinions is a great way for a child, or anyone for that matter, to discover that they have something worthwhile to say, something others will enjoy reading. By writing about themselves, children discover their unique voice.

HAVE FIVE MINUTES?

➤ "But, I don't know what to write about." Are these the first words you hear when your child sits down to complete an essay assignment? If so, spend a few minutes getting him to talk about his life. Discuss recent events, funny happenings, unfortunate accidents or scrapes, special occasions or celebrations, hopes—anything that might be of concern. Help him to see that his life is made up of hundreds of things he could write about.

➤ In this TV and movie age, children sometimes get the impression that "good stuff" has to contain intergalactic fights, murder, or outlandish feats (like keeping a home safe from burglars while your parents are vacationing in Europe). No wonder they have a hard time recognizing that their own lives are interesting. If this is the case with your third grader, pick a subject with which everyone is familiar, something as simple as, say, eating breakfast. Tell your child your own experience on the topic:

> My brothers ate cold cereal every day. They would race to the cupboard to be the first one to grab the cereal box. The first one, you see, got to read the back of the box while he munched on Cheerios or Corn Pops. Problem was, they never agreed on who was first. Me, I ate a single boiled egg (soft boiled with runny yoke and pepper) on toast each morning, wondering why my mother didn't give in and buy two boxes of cereal just to stop the squabbling.

> Often, telling your own experience will prompt your child to think about the uniqueness of his experience.

➤ Suggest that your child keep a journal or diary, but don't impose the "write every day" rule. If your child gets behind, he may give the activity up. For this reason, too, it is better not to purchase diaries (one year or five years) that are previously dated. Remind your third grader that he need not record *every* detail.

➤ Keep a family journal. Place a notebook someplace where everyone tends to hang out. Encourage all family members to record funny quotes, opinions, and memorable family events. Keep the format loose, so that everyone feels free to write often. You will be amazed and touched by this family record.

HAVE MORE TIME?

➤ Choose a time once a week (or even every day) where everyone in the family writes for ten minutes. Tell your family that they can write on any topic, that the writing can be gibberish but everyone's pencil must keep moving. If your third grader gets stuck, suggest he write: "I don't know what to write," until he has a new thought. Or suggest he make a list. At the end of the session, ask if anyone would like to share something—a word, a sentence, or the whole piece. Practice this activity a few times and you may be surprised at the number of times your child insists on continuing. You also may discover that you have more to write about than you ever knew.

Stories

Nothing empowers a young writer more than writing a story. When a child discovers that he can create a world entirely to his own liking; that he can create characters, put them in hot water, and get them out again; that when he hears others laugh or sigh or applaud because of *his* story—well, he has experienced true magic.

This year, your child will probably spend a good deal of time discussing story form. Although stories seem as unlimited as the imagination, they do have predictable structures. This structure includes a beginning, a middle, and an end. It also includes a problem and a solution. And in the most satisfying stories, the main character experiences some sort of change. Without this structure, the reader is cheated. The reader may not know why it's not a good story, but he knows that his expectations have not been met.

As your child stretches his writing muscles this year, help him to think about story elements: setting, characters, problem, and solution.

HAVE FIVE MINUTES?

➤ *Listen to this!* Let that be a familiar cry in your house. Read aloud passages you come across in books, magazines, or the newspaper that describe a character or a setting especially well. Follow with comments such as Can't you imagine this setting? Don't you feel like you know this character?

➤ Before writing a story, suggest to your child that he complete the Story Map on page 217. (You can photocopy this map or have him quickly sketch his own.)

➤ Encourage your child to tell you his story before he begins writing. Telling a story is especially effective for third graders who are easily distracted or become caught up in details of their own wonderful invention. Talking and listening to the effect of his words also gives a child confidence in his own voice as a writer. If your child begins to ramble, you can pull him in by saying, "Oh, the problem in this story is . . . I can't wait to see how you solve it."

➤ Third graders are notorious for writing bed-to-bed stories. In other words, they begin with the character waking up, they include every detail of the character's day (brushing teeth, putting on shoes, choosing something for breakfast) and will eventually end with the end of the character's day—if they don't give up first! If your child seems to be stuck in the bed-to-bed pattern, help him to see how professional writers deal with time. One way to begin is to point out that we almost never read about a character using the john, though we assume that they do! As you read aloud, study the first sentences of paragraphs that move the reader ahead in time:

> After school, Katy . . .
> That night, Katy . . .
> Three days passed before Katy . . .

HAVE MORE TIME?

➤ Some children feel more confident when they know exactly where they are going. You can give your child an effective story-telling structure by reading him *pourquoi*, or *why*, stories. These are imaginary stories that explain why the natural world is the way it is. Rudyard Kipling is best known for his "Just So" stories in which he explains how the camel got his hump or how the leopard got his spots. After reading *pourquoi* tales, suggest that your child try writing his own. He might want to begin by explaining certain traits of the family pet.

Pourquoi Tales
- *How Music Came to the World: An Ancient Mexican Myth,* by Hal Ober (Houghton Mifflin)
- *How the Animals Got Their Colors: Animal Myths from Around the World,* by Michael Rosen (Harcourt Brace)
- *How the Guinea Fowl Got Her Spots: A Swahili Tale of Friendship,* by Barbara Knutsen (Carolrhoda)
- *How the Leopard Got His Spots and Other Just So Stories,* by Rudyard Kipling (Dover)
- *How the Sea Began: A Taino Myth,* by George Crespo (Clarion)
- *How the Stars Fell into the Sky: A Navajo Legend,* by Jerrie Oughton (Houghton Mifflin)

Poetry

Many children develop a love of writing and a newfound confidence when they attempt to write poetry. Powerful imagery, imaginative associations, and stunning metaphors that seem so elusive to adult writers often come easily to the young. And because poetry must be shorter, or can be written by following a certain structure, it often appeals to the reluctant writer.

HAVE FIVE MINUTES?

➤ Look for poetry everywhere. Children become engaged in poetry through singing, chanting, rapping, and even dancing. Have your child make up new verses to favorite songs, raps, chants, jump-rope jingles, or poems.

➤ Read *Joyful Noise; Poems for Two Voices* by Paul Fleishman (Harper-Collins). These wonderful poems about insects are divided into two columns. You read one voice (one column) alternating with your child who reads the other.

➤ Many third graders still assume poetry must rhyme. Find examples of poems that don't rhyme and share them with your child. *For the Love of the Game: Michael Jordan and Me* by Eloise Greenfield (HarperCollins) and *Light and Shadow* by Myra Cohn Livingston (Holiday House) are two books written with free verse that appeal to eight- and nine-year-olds. (For more recommended poetry books see the list on page 113.)

➤ Buy a rhyming dictionary. To children who like to write rhyming verse, nothing is more valuable than a rhyming dictionary. One good one for third graders is *The Scholastic Rhyming Dictionary* by Sue Young (Scholastic).

➤ Create poetry performances. Have your child choose background music to accompany the reading of a poem. Or have your child make up a dance to go with a piece of poetry.

➤ Have your child write a poem using onomatopoeia, which means words such as *buzz, ring, growl,* that actually make the sound they represent. Brainstorm as many as you can think of (animal sounds are a good way to begin).

➤ Find examples of alliteration in the poetry you read together. Alliteration is when several words in a phrase begin with the same sound and is used to create a pleasant, musical tone. "The seals sleep silently on silver waves" is an example of alliteration.

➤ Suggest writing a cinquain, a five-line stanza consisting of two words in the first line, four words in the second, six words in the third, eight words in the fourth, and then back to two words in the last line. Here is a cinquain composed by a third grader:

> Mouse droppings
> Trailing across the floor
> Soon the trap will be set
> Don't eat that cheese chunk little mouse!
> Go Free

Writing a cinquain is a good alternative for children who balk at writing free verse. It often provides the success that then prompts children to try other forms of poetry.

HAVE MORE TIME?

➤ The best way to help your child develop talent as a poet is to read lots of poetry. Read a single poem aloud many times, each time giving it a slightly different interpretation. (You can do this by putting the emphasis on different words each time. See how many ways you can say the sentence: I never get what I want.)

➤ Choose books that represent different poetic styles and make comparisons. Then ask, What makes these poems different? Which style do you like better? Why did you pick that one?

Reports

Your own memory of report writing may involve choosing a topic and copying text straight from the encyclopedia. If you were really clever, you opened several different encyclopedias and copied some text from each. But eventually this method failed you. Teachers started talking about plagiarism and the need to write in your own words. They began insisting on primary sources. They began insisting that you *think*.

As an alternative to this route, you can help your third grader develop some report writing skills from the start. Develop a few simple skills this year, and each year your child will add a few more to his repertoire.

Poetry

- *A Child's Garden of Verses,* by Robert Lewis Stevenson (Abrams, Dutton)
- *Cricket Never Does: A Collection of Haiku and Tanka,* by Myra Cohn Livingston (Margaret McElderry)
- *Hoops,* by Robert Burleigh (Harcourt Brace)
- *Earth Always Endures: Native American Poems,* by Neil Philip (Viking)
- *Food Fight,* by Michael J. Rosen (Harcourt Brace)
- *Harlem,* by Walter Dean Myers (Scholastic Press)
- *Home on the Range,* by Paul Janeczko (Dial)
- *In Daddy's Arms I Am Tall,* edited by Javaka Steptoe (Lee & Low)
- *A Jar of Tiny Stars: Poems by NCTE Award-Winning Poets,* edited by Bernice Cullinan (Boyd Mills)
- *Roald Dahl's Revolting Rhymes* (Puffin)
- *Prayers from the Ark,* translated by Rumer Godden (Puffin)
- *Ten-Second Rainshowers: Poems by Young People,* compiled by Sandford Lyne (Simon & Schuster)
- *When Whales Exhale and Other Poems by Young People,* by Constance Levy (McElderry)

Writing a report involves four steps:
1. Choosing a topic
2. Gathering information
3. Organizing the information
4. Writing the report in one's own words

HAVE FIVE MINUTES?

➤ If your child has not been assigned a report topic, encourage him to choose a subject in which he is truly interested. A topic that fascinates him will certainly make the process more fun.

➤ To help your third grader gather and organize information, see the activities in Study Skills, page 96, if you haven't done so already. In addition to those strategies, try some of these:

- **Info Web** Have your child write his topic in the center of the page. Then encourage him to brainstorm everything he knows about it. Show him how to cluster information that relates by drawing separate "branches" from the center circle. Have him add to the web as he gathers new information.

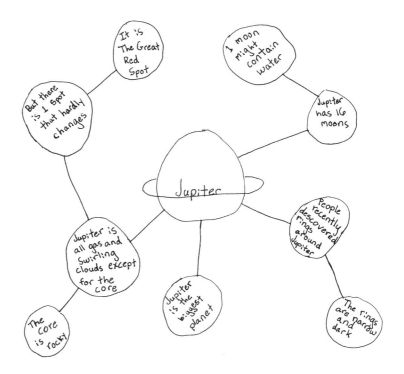

- Where could your third grader get information other than the encyclopedia? Spend some time brainstorming other possible sources.
  Your list might include books, magazine articles, and people who are
  knowledgeable on the topic. Is there a local expert on the topic in
  your town? If your child has computer access, perhaps he can find
  information on the Internet.
- Suggest your child think about his audience for the report. What
  kinds of information would be interesting to the reader?

➤ Talk about the facts as you and your child read, and see if any natural categories arise. For instance, on a report about a state, you might find that
the information falls into categories of geography, history, and symbols.
Write the categories as headings on three sheets of paper. Encourage
your third grader to record information on the appropriate sheets. Later,
help him to think about how he would like to order the three categories
in his report, and in what order the specific facts from each heading
should be written. This is a difficult task for third graders who will benefit
from your participation.

➤ To help your child to process the information, and write about it in his
own words, have him tell you about it ahead of time. Ask questions to
help him keep a focus on his audience and what the audience needs to
know.

Revision

Revision is the essence of writing. It is the stage
when the author stands back and looks at her writing
with an objective eye. Now is the time to ask: Is my
meaning clear? Have I presented the information in
the best order? Have I said all that I need to say?
Could I have said it with fewer words? Have I met my
purpose of entertaining (or informing)?

Learning to revise takes time and maturity. Most
third graders, when asked to revise, jump ahead to
editing. They don't mind correcting their work by
adding punctuation or fixing a spelling word. But
because they are such sequential writers, adding one
concrete event to another (remember the bed-to-bed
stories?), it is hard for them to imagine that more
experienced writers actually move their text around,

QUESTION, QUESTION

By far the best approach to help
children revise is to talk to them about
their writing. Tell your child, each and
every time, what works well in her piece.
Mention the growth you see. Question
your child when you do not understand
something, or if information appears to
be missing, or if you simply want to know
more. If you question your child
regularly, she will begin to keep her
audience in mind while she writes. Making
changes as she writes is a sophisticated
form of revision.

add or delete ("You want me to take something out?"), or even begin again in an entirely different way.

Nevertheless, third grade is a good time to reinforce the idea that the writing process is seldom complete after the first words have been recorded. In order to communicate effectively, writers must take the time to put themselves in the reader's place. If discussions about revision do not occur at this stage, children begin to place more emphasis on editing the mechanics of a written piece than they do the content of their writing. Although their writing might look neater and more informed initially, this overvaluing of the mechanics will no doubt shortchange the student's growth as a writer.

Good writing requires risk-taking. The more you help your child realize that the goal of writing is not perfection but the desire to express oneself in the most effective way, the more you will support her learning in this area. Here are some ways to begin.

HAVE FIVE MINUTES?

➤ Go ahead and revise the books that you read aloud together. Don't be afraid to say, "I would have used the word 'peeked' instead of 'looked'." Or, "This beginning is dull. I would have begun the story when the elephant said . . ." Get your child to join in on the act. Ask him, "Did you like that ending? How would you have ended this book instead?" Before long, your child will demonstrate the knowledge that stories can (and should) be improved upon.

➤ Ask your child to read her writing aloud. Many times a writer will catch places in the text that are unclear or out of order while reading it out loud. More experienced writers will even begin to hear places that could be stronger in word choice or details.

➤ Have your child brainstorm a list of titles for his piece and then choose the one he likes best. This helps him develop the concept that writers explore different ideas before making a choice.

➤ **Self-interview** The next time your third grader slaps her pencil down and shouts "Done," have her stop and ask herself a series of questions about her writing. Here are some she might use:
  • Does my story (article, learning log, letter) make sense?
  • Have I given the reader enough information?
  • Have I given more information than the reader needs?
  • Do I have an exciting beginning?
  • Do I end in a satisfying place?

➤ Show your child how to revise his writing with the use of a computer. Children are much more apt to add or delete text, or move text around, when they know that their changes won't require hours of copying work over by hand. They can try revisions in the word processing program, and if they don't like them, they can return the text to its original state. They can even keep several drafts of the same story for comparison. (Third graders love to get their classmates to vote on which approach they like best.) If you don't have access to a computer, see if your child's school or the local library provides computers for public use.

Perhaps most important, find out what the teacher expects in written work. Does the teacher encourage children to revise the content of their stories? If so, she is probably downright enthusiastic when your child crosses out words, adds new text, or rewrites the first line. If, however, your child has a teacher who values neat, correctly edited drafts above all else, you may have difficulty convincing your child that revision is a good thing. Talk to your child's teacher. Perhaps she recognizes the value of revision but fears parents' responses to "sloppy drafts." Since it is nearly impossible for third graders to concentrate on penmanship, strong content, and mechanics all at one time (and most third graders find copying final drafts torture), see if you can't agree on some revision techniques that would satisfy both of you. Here are some ways third graders can make changes:

- Carets (^) for inserting text above a line
- Arrows for showing where text should be moved to
- Asterisks for marking where a large block of text should be added
- Spiderlegs—this is what teachers call taping additions to pages
- Lines through words for deletions

Editing

By the third grade, most children realize that writing must follow standard conventions—words must be spelled correctly, punctuation must be correct, sentences must be grammatically correct—or others won't be able to read or understand what has been written.

As children master the conventions, they naturally incorporate them in their writing. However, every new skill requires time before it is used with consistency. Just because your child has been introduced to quotation marks doesn't mean they will appear with the dialogue in the next draft. Mastery requires lots and lots of practice. (Of course, the more your child reads, the more she will be exposed to writing conventions.)

When teaching your child a new skill, or drawing attention to a previously introduced skill, it is best to wait until she has completed an entire draft. Most third graders cannot simultaneously concentrate on developing ideas, organizing them, writing them with attention to creative detail, and paying attention to writing conventions. (In fact, most professional writers can't write and edit at the same time, either.) Let your child record her ideas, respond to them with enthusiasm (a very important step), and then help her to clean up her draft.

This year, it is appropriate for your third grader to edit with attention to
- punctuation
- paragraph formation (end of the year skill)
- grammar
- spelling

Punctuation

If third graders spend a good deal of time reading, knowing what the different punctuation marks on the page mean should come easily. Do they remember to use these marks in their own writing? Well, that's another story! Generally, third graders are expected to
- use capital letters at the beginning of sentences and for proper nouns
- use end punctuation (period, question mark, exclamation point)
- use an apostrophe with possessives
- use commas in a series
- use quotation marks when writing dialogue

EDITING ACRONYM

Suggest that your child remember the word "cup" when editing his work.

C—capital letters at the beginning of each sentence.
U—uppercase letters for names of people and places.
P—punctuation at the end of the sentence.

If your child can remember this acronym, he can proofread his own work any time, any place.

HAVE FIVE MINUTES?

➤ After the funnies have been read on Sunday, choose a different punctuation mark and have your child highlight or circle as many as he can find in his favorite comic strips. If your child is interested, suggest he try writing his own comic strip. (Comic strips are short and therefore a good form to use when concentrating on punctuation.)

➤ One of the best ways to help children learn how to use commas in a series is to have them write a list first. Next, suggest that your child put the list into a sentence. Show her how to use commas to separate the items in her list.

➤ To practice writing possessives, have your third grader pull five things out of your junk drawer. Suggest she write a paragraph telling about the five things she found. Ask her to identify the owners of the objects in her paragraph.

HAVE MORE TIME?

➤ Some children really appreciate having an "editor's checklist." Make several photocopies of the checklist on pages 218–19. After your third grader has written a first draft, she can return to see if she has included the necessary writing conventions, checking each requirement off as she goes.

Paragraph Form

Using paragraph form is a skill that may not be introduced to your third grader until the end of the year. As your child becomes a more proficient writer, you will want to point out proper paragraph form.

• When you read aloud, show your child how groups of sentences are clustered. Tell him that each cluster is called a paragraph and that each paragraph tells about a single main idea. When an author wants to introduce a new idea, he begins a new paragraph.

• Open a page to a book. Encourage your child to show you where each paragraph on that page begins and ends. Help him to see that the first sentence of each new paragraph is indented.

• The next time you read fiction together, point out that every time a new character speaks, the dialogue is written on a new line. Suggest that your child apply this rule to his own writing.

• If your child plans to write an essay or a nonfiction report, suggest he web the information ahead of time to see how the paragraphs could be organized. For a description of webbing, or for more activities on recognizing main ideas, see "Reports," page 113, and "Summarize," page 85.

Grammar

What is the best way to teach your child to speak and write customary English? Should you teach him proper sentence structure—that is, subjects, simple subjects, and predicates? Should you drill him in parts of speech: nouns, pronouns, adjectives, verbs? Should you teach your third grader about irregular verbs? Verb tenses? (Perhaps, you think, you'd better take a refresher course yourself.)

You could study grammar with your child, but it is likely that you would be wasting precious moments—moments that could be spent helping your child develop a genuine understanding of language and how it is constructed.

Teaching children of primary school age about grammar through the use of worksheets or English skill workbooks is ineffective. Young children are simply unable to apply these exercises to their own speaking and writing. In fact, teaching grammar as an isolated skill may even have negative effects. Children who struggle with understanding the difference between adjectives and adverbs often suffer a loss in their confidence as writers or get thoroughly bored. Kids who heretofore wrote with verve suddenly say, "I'm terrible at Language Arts." And perhaps worst of all, time spent on filling in blanks on worksheets could have been spent reading and writing—activities that have been proven to help children acquire a greater understanding of grammar. For these reasons, many school systems do not begin teaching formal grammar until children are in junior high or even high school and have had more practice in looking at their writing from many angles.

But, you say, children need these skills. Children must learn to speak and write correctly! And that is absolutely true. Children need to understand that their writing will be difficult to read if they don't write in complete sentences, or if their sentences go on and on for pages. They need to know that words are tools, and that the right word (especially verbs) can engage the reader. They need to know that the use of incorrect negatives—"There weren't no flowers" or "I won't never climb mountains"—confuses readers. By encouraging your child to write, and by responding to his writing as a helpful mentor, you can help your child develop the skills he requires. Here are some specific suggestions.

> ## I OR ME?
>
> Does your child have trouble deciding when to use "me" and when to use "I"? Is it "Will and me" are going outside or "Will and I"? If so, suggest he say the sentence to himself with only "I" or "me." For example: "Me is going outside" or "I am going outside." This should help clear up the confusion.

HAVE FIVE MINUTES?

➤ After your third grader has read his latest story or essay to you, respond by telling him what works: "I loved that sentence about seeing the faces of wild, but friendly animals in your knotty-pine paneling. It reminded me of a summer cabin I used to visit when I was a kid. I used to see faces in the wall, too." Then, question your child about sections of his piece that may not be working well: "You wrote 'Helps me look in the closet and under my bed.' But I didn't understand *who* helps you. Could you give me more information?"

➤ Use the language of grammar, without insisting that your child memorize it. For instance, when suggesting that your child choose a more exact word, you might say, "You wrote, 'I got up onto the wall.' Could you choose a different *verb*, such as climbed or hoisted, that might show me exactly what it was like to scale that wall?" Or you might simply name a word in passing: "Oh, you wrote the word 'expertly,' that's a good *adverb* to describe your climb." (For more suggestions on how to help your child use precise language, see "Synonyms and Antonyms," page 90.)

➤ Demonstrate the ineffectiveness of a runaway sentence. Write one long sentence, without punctuation, to describe what you need to do before going to bed:

> First I have to put in a load of laundry so Janey will have her gymnastics leotard and then I will pay some bills and then I will put on my pajamas and wash up and brush my teeth and read for awhile then I will turn out the light.

> Read your sentence to your third grader without taking a breath. Then discuss how the run-on sentence could be broken up into several sentences. Use transitional words such as "before" and "after" to make the paragraph easier to understand.

➤ Point out occasions when your child suddenly switches verb tense when writing. Say, for instance, "You wrote 'I saw many kinds of snakes.' But later, you wrote, 'I see a boa constrictor.' Are you writing about something that happened in the past? Or are you telling the story as it is happening?" And then, "Which word do you need to change?"

HAVE MORE TIME?

➤ If your child likes to write poetry, he might enjoy learning this structure—one that also requires him to recognize parts of speech.
> one noun
> two adjectives
> three verbs ending in ing
> two adjectives
> a noun connecting back to line 1

For instance:
> cat
> black, sleek
> yawning, stretching, posing
> aloof, patient
> queen

➤ Third graders also love Mad Libs, a game in which they fill in blanks with random nouns, verbs, and adjectives to compose silly paragraphs. You might want to pick up a commercial pad of Mad Libs or try composing and swapping some of your own.

Spelling

The ability to use conventional spelling is measured by question 1 on the Reading Assessment, and questions J and K on the Writing Assessment.

Spelling is often an area of concern for parents of third graders because the errors are so visible. You may not know for sure if your child understands what an adjective is, or how to structure a paragraph, but you do know that every third word in your child's written work remains misspelled!

Rest assured, spelling errors are still the norm for third grade. Children at this age *are* consolidating what they know about spelling, but that consolidation still requires a good deal of trial and error. Your child probably knows that both the phonogram "ee" and the phonogram "ea" make the long *e* sound, but is the word "treet" or "treat"? Is it "lite" or "light"? "Friend" or "freind"? Keeping it all straight is still tough for the average eight- or nine-year-old.

Phonics, the tool your child uses to decode new words, is critical for developing good spelling sense. As children learn about letter clusters called phonograms ("igh" is a phonogram, so is "ie") they begin to see patterns. Suddenly the words "light," "sight," and "night" are not viewed as words with random clusters of letters, but as words that follow predictable sequences. Hopefully, the spelling lists your child receives at school are occasionally composed of phonetic word families in addition to words that children frequently misspell when writing.

Here are some ways that you can help your child grow into a more competent speller at home.

HAVE FIVE MINUTES?

➤ If your child is having trouble with one or more of the common phonograms (letter combinations—see box), write words that follow the same pattern on an index card or on a wall chart. Write the phonograms in a different color. Remind her that she can refer to this to check her spelling. Before long she'll have the patterns memorized.

➤ Children tend to be fairly consistent in their spelling errors. Look for patterns in the mistakes your third grader makes. Does she forget that many words require a silent *e*? Does she substitute *o* for *a* in words like "wall," "tall," "fall"? Once you recognize a pattern, you can give her the information she needs.

PHONICS

Here are some letter combinations that many third graders need further help in learning:

- igh — as in night, light, sight
- eigh — as in neighbor, weigh, freight
- ough — as in fought, bought, thought
- ough — as though
- ough — as in through
- ough — as in enough
- ould — as in could, would, should
- augh — as in caught, taught, fraught
- augh — as in laugh
- vowels with r — as in hurt, work, bird, fern
- double consonants — as in rabbit, happen, button, yellow
- le — as in little, able, apple
- silent letters — as in walk, ghost, knight

➤ Give your child a list of words that have a consistent phonetic element—for example: knife, knock, knuckle, knight. Encourage her to not only identify the common phonetic element in the list but to tell you what she knows about it: "All of those words begin with 'kn'. The *k* is always silent."

➤ When your child wants to write a word that she doesn't know how to spell, suggest she try writing it on her own. If the word is spelled incorrectly, talk her through the correct spelling. Here is a typical conversation that might occur between a child and parent.

"How do you spell friction?"
"Give it a try, then I'll help."
(Child writes) fricshon
"Great job. The first four letters are correct. But the sh sound you hear in friction doesn't come from the letters *sh*. Which letters create the sh sound in words like fiction, dictionary, or suction?"
"ti?"
"Yes. So show me how you would spell the word now." (If the child

did not recall "ti," then the parent would teach the child that phonogram.)

If the word does not follow any discernible spelling pattern, help your child develop her own way of memorizing the correct spelling (see page 125 for suggestions).

➤ After your child has written a rough draft, suggest she circle three words that she knows are spelled incorrectly. You'll be surprised how often the three words contain the same spelling mistake. Help your child to spell the words correctly using the method describe above.

➤ If needed, review the spelling of contractions. Although your child has no doubt been exposed to contractions in school, sometimes it's helpful to reinforce this knowledge one-on-one. Show her that a contraction is a short way of saying or writing two or more words. Letters are dropped when the words are combined, and an apostrophe is used to mark their place. To give your child practice in writing contractions, write a note to her using the more formal two words. Then challenge her to rewrite the note using contractions. Here is a list of contractions to choose from:

I am/I'm	were not/weren't
he is/he's	I would/I'd
she is/she's	are not/aren't
cannot/can't	let us/let's
will not/won't	who is/who's
could not/couldn't	is not/isn't
should not/shouldn't	had not/hadn't
was not/wasn't	

➤ Teach your child the sing-song rule: *I before e except after c. Or when sounded like a as in neighbor or weigh.*

➤ Don't be lulled into thinking that spelling can be mastered by studying all the rules and patterns. The English language is nothing if not unpredictable. Many common words are exceptions to the rules. Knowing the spelling of these words requires only one thing: memorization. On page 202 are the seventy-four most frequently misspelled words. Challenge your child to spell ten at a time. Keep a list of those words she needs further help with.

Later, suggest that your child try a number of these ways to memorize those words and/or the words she brings home from school:

• Use the "Look, Say, Write" system. Look at the word and trace the letters with your fingers. Then say the word while you copy it onto a sheet of paper. Now cover the word and try to write it without look-ing. Check your spelling.

- Write each word three times.
- Look for smaller words within the word. The word "tomorrow," for example, has three; tom or row.
- Create acrostics. Write your spelling word vertically. Then write a new word beginning with each letter of your spelling word. For example, here is an acrostic for the word "barrel":

> **b**ossy
> **a**nteater
> **r**unning
> **r**apidly
> **e**ating
> **l**asagna

- Ask someone to write your spelling words with only the vowels (use lines to mark where the consonants go). See if you can fill in the miss-ing letters. Or, if you have difficulty remembering vowels, have some-one write only the consonants.
- Write the words in alphabetical order.
- Make a crossword puzzle using the words.
- See how many words you can connect by sharing letters (in the same way words are connected on a Scrabble board).

➤ Help your child memorize words using mnemonic devices such as "He is a fri<u>end</u> to the end" or the "Princi<u>pal</u> is your pal." Encourage her to make up her own associations to memorize the real sticklers.

HAVE MORE TIME?

➤ If your child brings home a weekly spelling list, does all of the required activities, but still gets a number of the words wrong on Friday's test, she may not be capitalizing on her personal learning style. Some children learn best when information is presented visually, others learn better when the information is presented auditorally or kinesthetically (touch). (For a list of books about learning styles see "Questions and Answers About Third Grade," page 27.) If your child is not meeting success, sug-gest that she choose one or more strategies from this list:

VISUAL STRATEGIES
- Write the word in one color. Then close your eyes and visualize the word in that color.
- Write each letter of the word in a different color.

- Write the word in large letters on an index card. Cut around the word so you can see the shape of the word.

- Write the word in colored chalk on the pavement. Then use a hose or sprinkling can to erase the word letter by letter.
- Find the word in magazines, newspapers, or junk mail. Circle it or cut it out.
- Paint the word on a large sheet of newspaper or poster board.

KINESTHETIC OR TACTILE STRATEGIES

- Write the word in shaving cream, salt on a cookie sheet, sand, or mud.
- Tap a pencil as you say the letters.
- March in place while you spell the word.
- Write the word in huge letters in the air.
- Use magnetic letters or letter tiles from Scrabble to spell the word.
- Spell the word with a glitter glue pen. Let the word dry. Then close your eyes and trace the letters with your finger. Guess what the word is.
- Use a flashlight to spell the word on a darkened wall.
- Have someone trace the letters of a word on your back. Guess what the word is. Then switch roles.
- Draw the word in giant letters on the pavement (or use masking tape on the floor). Walk, skip, or hop along the letters.
- Form the word with clay letters.

AUDITORY STRATEGIES

- Say the word slowly, emphasizing the letter sounds. If a word has silent letters, you might want to sound them out (*k-nife*) so that you will remember them.
- As you write the word, say each letter aloud.
- Sing the word to a familiar tune:
  l-i-g-h-t, l-i-g-h-t, l-i-g-h-t
  and light is the word-o.

Oral Presentations

Third grade is apt to be the year when children make their first oral presentation. They may be asked to give a book report, a literature group summary, a presentation on a social studies report, or a science fair project. Depending on your child's personality, the thought of giving an oral presentation may bring excitement or paralyzing panic. Either way, here are a few tips to help your budding public speaker be a hit with his class.

HAVE FIVE MINUTES?

➤ Many beginning speakers associate a long presentation with a well-done presentation. Help your child to see that it is the choice of topic and fascinating information that impresses an audience rather than length. You can do this by giving mock presentations of your own. The first presentation would, of course, go on and on with boring or irrelevant data while the second presentation, on the same topic, would be brief and contain a few lively, juicy facts.

➤ Help your third grader organize his presentation. If he is going to give an oral book report or a literature group summary, you may want to suggest that he complete one of the graphic organizers found on pages 216–17. If it is a science or social studies presentation, suggest he use props such as magazine pictures, charts, maps, or actual objects to keep himself on track during his presentation. He can place his props in a particular order and use them to guide his thinking and speaking.

➤ Suggest that your child practice his presentation at home first. Respond to his talk in the same way you would his writing. Tell him what he is doing well first. Be as specific as possible so he can repeat his success. Then tell him one or two things he might improve, such as the volume of his voice. Giving too much critical feedback at one time will likely hurt his performance rather than improve it. It takes a good deal of experience to evolve into a good oral speaker.

➤ If your child has a flexible third-grade teacher, he may be able to use one of the following formats as an alternative to the traditional book report. The beauty of these formats is that they not only get kids really thinking about the books they've read, but they may be easier for children who are shy or self-conscious when talking in class. Sometimes it can be easier to play the role of a book character than oneself.

INSTEAD OF A BOOK REPORT

- Present a television commercial convincing others to read the book
- Present a puppet show of several scenes from the book
- Present an interview with one of the book's characters
- Draw a series of illustrations for the story (if not illustrated) and show them while giving the report
- Make a chart that compares this book to another book the class has read; share the chart with the class
- Write and read a letter to the main character discussing events from the story

Cursive Writing

When asked, most children say that what they want to learn in third grade is cursive writing. Cursive is a marvelous, connected code, known only to those who have traveled beyond the second grade.

The joy they anticipate may, however, quickly dissipate when the reality of learning new symbols, reconditioning small hand muscles, and endless hours of writing practice begin. If your third grader's enthusiasm for learning cursive writing has begun to wane, here are a few recommendations for giving him a boost.

Before you attempt to do any cursive writing support at home, ask your child's teacher for a copy of the alphabet chart from the program she teaches. If your child is learning D'Nelian, you do not want to teach him the Palmer method—no matter how fond you are of the loopy letters. Teaching a handwriting system that differs from the one used in the school will cause your child to become confused and frustrated.

HAVE MORE TIME?

➤ Find out why your child finds handwriting difficult. If he says, "I just can't see how the letters are supposed to go," you will want to use a different strategy than if he says, "My hand hurts when I write cursive," or "I just can't remember how to make the letters." After you have gathered information try these.

FOR SIGHT DIFFICULTIES

- Have your child's eyes checked.
- If your child copies letters from the chalkboard at school, see if copying from a nearby paper is easier. If so, share this information with your child's teacher.

- When you give your child a word to copy, write each letter in a different color.

FOR FINE MOTOR DIFFICULTIES

- Make sure your child is holding her pencil in a manner that is not too tiring. You may want to purchase a pencil grip for proper finger placement, or mold a grip from a piece of clay or putty.
- Ask your child to draw continuous ocean waves, or smoke coming from a chimney in order to practice the up and down or circular motion of cursive writing.
- Play relaxing music while your child writes to relieve some of the tension.
- Make the letter your child is learning first. Then have your child trace over your letter several times.

FOR DIFFICULTY IN REMEMBERING LETTER FORMATION

- Suggest that your child draw large cursive letters on the sidewalk or driveway with chalk.
- Give your child a large paintbrush and a bucket of water. Have her form letters on the outside wall of your home.
- Give your child some pipe cleaners with which to mold individual letters.
- Encourage your child to "walk" the letter in your living room before writing it. Have him say the name of the letter as he walks it.
- Talk your child through the formation of a letter as he writes it: "begin at the base line, hump, hump, hump, serif" for the letter *m*. When your child has memorized the sequence, encourage him to talk himself through the motions if necessary.

- Give your child practice in reading cursive. Write him brief notes and leave them on the refrigerator, in his lunchbox, on his pillow at night.

Reading and Writing Enrichment

When it comes to reading and writing, even the highest achievers can lose ground during the middle grade years. Third and fourth grade are increasingly social years. The importance of family time begins to recede and is replaced with dates with friends, sports, activities, and clubs. Reading, often considered a solitary activity, gives way to chatting—on the phone, on the computer, with anyone in the room.

No matter how quiet a third grade classroom is expected to be, social activity is bubbling just below the surface. Children whisper, pass notes, and communicate with eye and body language. Teachers capitalize on this need to connect. They channel social energy into productive work. Children meet to discuss their favorite books. They study character, plot, and setting in cooperative learning groups. They teach one another during peer writing conferences, and they share reading and writing strategies in class meetings. By making reading and writing a social activity, the wise teacher is making it a valued activity.

When reading is not social, it is viewed as an activity for "brains," or "misfits." For this reason, children who heretofore excelled at reading and writing may begin to hide or ignore their proficiency. If a third grader is being pulled out of her regular class for quiet, individual work with a specialist, she may begin to resent this treatment and may try to sabotage it. On the other hand, if a group of children are attending a gifted and talented program that is lively and social, they will thrive.

And here lies the challenge at home. How can you best support your talented reader and/or writer? By creating social times around reading and writing. Children who have the opportunity to participate in hobbies with their parents gain important skills. They develop passions that can last a lifetime. Make reading and writing a social hobby in your home. Keep your child challenged. Keep the love alive.

HAVE FIVE MINUTES?

➤ Telling a third grader to "go read a book" can be the equivalent of telling the five-year-old that it's time for a nap. The last thing your child wants to do is go off where she might miss something. So keep books everywhere—on the kitchen counter, near every chair, and in the car. The next time she's just hanging out, she may be tempted to open one of those books and enter a world that is far more stimulating than simply waiting for something to happen.

➤ Place a "book" journal in a prominent place in your home. Encourage everyone in the family to write brief book critiques in it:

> 1/5/98 I just finished *My Father's Dragon*. This book is really silly, but fun. I liked how the boy kept outsmarting the animals by giving them something from his backpack and then sneaking off. You should read it.

➤ Or, instead of a "book" journal, begin a "famous words" journal. Have everyone record meaningful quotes or quirky language that they've heard and enjoyed. Don't forget to include the lively sayings your own family comes up with. When three-year-old Joey calls the back of knees "leg pits" or your third grader writes this sentence to include one of her spelling words, "When your get married, you say until <u>debt</u> do us part," write it down!

➤ As you read together, point out passages in which the author has used one of the five senses to create imagery. When does the author call upon the reader's sense of smell? Taste? Touch? Later, point out times when your child has drawn upon the senses to create effective imagery in her own writing.

➤ Introduce your child to the concept of the mood or tone of a story. Ask, "How does this story make you feel? Is the mood silly, suspenseful, scary?" Explore ways an author creates mood. The next time your child is busy writing in the car or at the kitchen table ask her what mood she is creating in her story.

➤Suggest that your child write a "stump your parents quiz." Encourage her to not only come up with a list of questions and answers that may boondoggle her parents, but to develop a response key. For instance:

Questions Answered Correctly	Result
From 1-3	Send these parents back to kindergarten
From 4-6	Help these parents brush up on your homework
From 7-10	Oh, oh. These parents are getting a little too clever for your own good. Keep an eye on them.

➤Of course, it's only fair that you should try to stump your third grader. To do so, send her on a dictionary scavenger hunt. Ask questions, such as "Where might you find moquette?" and "What does a pycnometer measure?"

➤Help your third grader differentiate between fact and opinion. Read a factual article and a letter to the editor on the same subject aloud. Then discuss which forum contained facts and which contained opinion. Discuss the purposes of both.

➤Encourage your child to write her autobiography. Suggest that she use photographs of herself with captions to create a book about her own history.

➤ Collect quotes from favorite books that you've read together. Then read the quotes at the dinner table and have family members guess what fictional or biographical characters said them. Encourage your third grader to collect quotes for future family quizzes.

➤ Suggest your child plan a real or fantasy trip. Propose that he write a letter requesting travel brochures and record sights and events of interest. Encourage him to use maps to determine a car or flight route. Help him to collect and read weather maps to determine what everyone should pack. If you can't actually go on this trip, take an imaginary trip at home. Plan a festive party with appropriate food and dress to celebrate the work your third grader did and the knowledge he learned.

➤ What type of fiction do you like to read? Mysteries? Science fiction? Adventure? Contemporary realism? Together, explore different genres by reading *But That's Another Story*, edited by Sandy Asher (Walker). This book contains stories of each genre along with a description of the genre and an author interview.

   Here are a few books your accomplished reader might enjoy.

Fiction

- *Arthur for the Very First Time*, by Patricia Maclaughlin (HarperCollins)
- *Bunnicula*, by Deborah and James Howe (Simon & Schuster)
- *Dear Mr. Henshaw*, by Beverly Cleary (Morrow)
- *Lily's Crossing*, by Patricia Reilly Giff (Bantam Doubleday Dell)
- *The Littles*, by John Peterson (Scholastic)
- *Sees Behind Trees*, by Michael Dorris (Hyperion)

Nonfiction

- *The Buck Stops Here*, by Alice Provensen (HarperCollins)
- *Magic Fun*, by Marilyn Baillie (Little, Brown)
- *Starry Messenger*, by Peter Sis (Farrar Straus Giroux)
- *The Way Things Work*, by David MacCauley (Houghton Mifflin)

Math Exercises

Problem Solving and Logic

The ability to approach problems in a variety of ways is measured by questions 1, 14, 18, 20, and 21 on the Math Assessment.

When you think of mathematical problem solving, does your mind suddenly leap to word problems such as:

> If train A was traveling a distance of 360 miles at the speed of 60 miles per hour, and train B was traveling 375 miles at the speed of 75 miles per hour, which train would reach its destination first?

Most of us equate problem solving with those exhilarating or dreaded word problems (depending on which side of the bell curve our grades fell on) that require math students to determine the *right* procedure for calculating the *right* answer.

Traditionally, students are taught to recognize words that act as clues for identifying the right procedure. In the problem above, the words "per hour" would suggest that division is the operation of choice. Unfortunately, for too many students, the question, What should I divide into what? would still remain.

Children who are inadvertently taught that the purpose of problem solving is to find the correct answer are placed at a disadvantage, particularly if opportunities to explore patterns, play with numbers, and develop problem solving strategies have been infrequent. Rather than matching words with abstract procedures, children need to develop confidence in their own abilities to puzzle a problem out—to try and fail, try and fail, try and perhaps succeed. They need to know that when it comes to problem solving their thinking is valued more than the correct answer. They need to feel it is safe to reveal their thinking to you and to their teachers so ideas can be further explored and understood.

Fortunately, the way in which problem solving is taught in today's schools is being examined all across the country. Math problems are not restricted to just testing students' ability to apply mathematical calculations, they are also used to teach children to think mathematically, to tackle real and complex problems in everyday lives, to discover for themselves how math is a universal system based on awesome patterns, and to experience genuine pleasure in their own ability to arrive at solutions.

It is crucial that children accept the idea that math problems can be solved by using many different approaches. For instance, when solving the train problem, one child might add $60 + 60 + 60 + 60 + 60 + 60$ and $75 + 75 + 75 + 75 + 75$ to determine that train b got to its destination first. Another child might draw a picture to determine how far each train could go if traveling 60 miles per hour, multiply the difference between 60 and 75 miles per hour, add the difference to the quotient, and then make a logical guess that train b will arrive first.

Books for Problem Solving Practice

- *The Case of the Missing Birthday Party,* by Joanne Rocklin (Cartwheel)
- *The Eleventh Hour,* by Graeme Base (Harry N. Abrams, Inc.)
- *Math Mini Mysteries,* by Sandra Markle (Atheneum)
- *Math Mysteries: Stories and Activities to Build Problem Solving Skills,* by Jack Silbert (Scholastic)
- *One Grain of Rice: A Mathematical Folktale,* by Demi (Scholastic)

Some may argue that these children are wasting their time and simply reinventing the wheel, that they could solve the problem faster and with greater ease if we just have them memorize a surefire procedure. But consider for a moment what is lost. While the first child works out the problem, he deepens his understanding that multiplication (6×60) is repeated addition (adding 60 six times). Perhaps he notices that the child who divided 360 by 60 got the same answer he did. Mmm, six. Now he's on his way to seeing relationships between multiplication and division. When taught this way, children learn mathematics in depth rather than breadth.

And what about the child who instantly recognizes that this problem can be solved by quick division, but due to a computation error determines that train *a* arrives at its destination first? Should this child be penalized for not coming up with the right answer? Or praised for choosing a strategy that works? Which response is likely to buoy the growing math student?

This is not to say that children should approach problem solving without instruction or guidance. Teachers and parents can provide children with a solid foundation of strategies and timely nudges to learn lifelong problem-solving skills. In fact, the parent is in the ideal position to help the child view herself as a competent mathematician. Here's how:

1. Create a spirit of mathematical exploration. Look for problems to solve together. Once you get started, you will find that they are all around you. Is there enough room to move your bed to that wall? How many hours will it take to get to Uncle John's? What is the probability that it will rain tomorrow?

2. Teach your child this sequence of problem solving: **Think** (What are you being asked to figure out?), **Plan** (How can you solve the problem?), **Solve** (Choose a strategy and give it a go.), **Look back** (Is your answer reasonable?) This last step is particularly important and often overlooked. Ask your child, "How could you check your answer?" Then encourage your child to see if the answer is in the ballpark.

3. Tell your child that often there are many ways to solve a problem, and that math problems, particularly those in real life, can have many answers. For instance, there are a number of solutions to the problem: What coins add up to twenty-five cents?

4. Value your child's thinking above all else. When your child comes up with a solution, respond with "Tell me how you got that." Do not ask this only when your child gives an incorrect answer. By encouraging your child to share her process, you will be given a unique view into how she thinks. More often than not, you will be amazed by her logic, whether she came up with the answer you expected or not. If she's harboring misconceptions, you'll know what to work on next.

5. Many children buckle the minute they hear a word problem. Words just swim in their heads. If your third grader would rather clean her room than listen to you present a problem, suggest she practice telling the problem back to you in her own words and/or creating a mental image of the problem. Then have her describe the image. Let her know that some problems take a good deal of time to solve. Remind her of how good it feels to arrive at a solution.

6. Whenever you are about to solve a problem, "think out loud" so she sees that there is nothing magical about the process. For example, you might say: "Let's see, this recipe calls for one third of a cup of sugar. My measuring cup only shows quarter measurements, there is no mark for one third. But I know that if I cut a piece of cake into thirds, one third would be more than one quarter and less than one half. So I'll just measure the sugar to somewhere between those two places."

7. The above example demonstrates the use of a simple problem (cutting a slice of cake into equal pieces) to figure out a more difficult one (how to measure a third cup of sugar). Beginning with an easier problem and making comparisons is a great strategy for solving problems. Here is a list of strategies mathematicians of all ages use to solve problems. You

may want to post this list on your refrigerator, but suggesting these approaches in not enough. You need to model these strategies (by thinking out loud and solving problems together) in order for your child to incorporate them into her own repertoire of problem-solving skills.

- Use objects
- Draw a picture
- Make a chart
- Make an organized list
- Look for a pattern
- Work backwards
- Think of a simpler problem
- Guess and check
- Use logical reasoning

You may be concerned that by giving your child oodles of time to come up with problem-solving solutions, she is losing valuable time learning basic mathematical skills. Fear not. Try some of the problems and activities suggested below, and see for yourself that problem solving is the best way for her to get painless practice in computation—and a firm grasp on mathematical concepts.

HAVE FIVE MINUTES?

➤ Search for patterns in everyday life. What natural events follow patterns? It may not take your third grader long to think of seasonal patterns, but what about storm patterns, tidal patterns, life cycle patterns? If she is constantly on the lookout for patterns, she will begin to recognize them in her math work, and she will come to understand that searching for patterns is a good way to solve many problems.

➤ The next time you are waiting for an appointment, write a sequence of numbers that follow a particular pattern. Ask your child to guess which number would come next in the sequence. Here are some examples:

    3, 6, 9, 12, 15, __   (18. This pattern is multiple of threes)
    2, 5, 4, 7, 6, 9, __   (8. This pattern is add three, subtract 1)
    1, 4, 5, 10, 20, __   (40. Each new number is the sum of the numbers
                            in the list.)

➤ Introduce your child to palindromes: "What do these numbers and words have in common: 6,446, dad, level, and 'A man, a plan, a canal, Panama!'" (Palindromes are words, numbers or phrases that remain the same when written in reverse.) Challenge your third grader to find all of the number palindromes between 1 and 100. What happens when you add a palindrome to a palindrome? What happens when you subtract a palindrome from a palindrome? Do you always get the same results? How do you know?

➤ Play Picky Petunia. Invent a logic problem such as "Picky Petunia loves books but she hates to read. She loves school, but she hates learning. She loves looking, but she hates to watch. What else does Petunia love?" Encourage your third grader to figure out the pattern by asking questions: "Does she like fishing?" In which you would answer, "No, she hates fishing but she loves hooks." When your child thinks she has figured out the rule, have her give an example of what Petunia loves and hates. (Petunia only loves words that contain "oo.") Then switch roles. Have your third grader give you a Picky Petunia problem.

➤ Give your child an equation without the arithmetic signs. For example:

3	4	5	12	$(3 + 4 + 5 = 12)$
6	3	5	8	$(6 - 3 + 5 = 8)$
9	3	2	12	$(9 - 3 \times 2 = 12)$

Challenge her to insert the correct signs to make the equation true. (This is a good problem to demonstrate the strategy called guess and check. Help your child to realize that she can use the information to make a logical guess. After she tries one possibility, she makes another guess based on what she learned from the first try. Every new guess should lead the problem solver closer to the solution.)

➤ Waiting in line at the grocers? Give your child coin challenges: "I'm thinking of five coins that equal 17¢. What are they? I'm thinking of five coins that equal 51¢. What are they?" Then have your third grader challenge you in the same way. If your child has difficulty coming up with solutions, give her pencil and paper when you get home. Show her how to make a chart or a list to keep track of the combinations she has already tried.

➤ Introduce math riddles and challenges at the dinner table. There are many books that offer wonderful riddles such as this one from *Tricky Twisters* (World Book): "If you were to see a cow in front of two cows, a cow behind two cows, and a cow between two cows, how many cows would you see altogether?" (You would see three cows standing in a line.)

➤ Give your child problems that begin with "How many ways . . ." For example, How many ways can you organize your closet? How many ways can you pack your lunch? How many ways can we schedule use of the family computer?

➤ If problems arise between siblings, ask the children to come up with solutions themselves. After each child offers a solution, say, "That's one way to solve the problem. Can you think of another one?" Continue until several solutions (hopefully one will be a win-win solution) can be found.

➤ Provide your third grader with an answer and have her come up with as many problems as she can. Here is one way to record those problems:

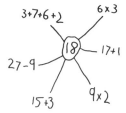

HAVE MORE TIME?

➤ Play strategic games with your child. A game such as chess helps develop analytical skills and helps a child to understand that problem solving takes time, concentration, and sometimes the necessity to start over. Another game that requires children to develop strategic and logical thinking is the Attribute Game. Use the templates on page 220 to make a set of attribute shapes. Here are the directions for the Attribute Game.

ATTRIBUTE GAME

1. Draw a Venn diagram on a large sheet of paper. (You can use two loops of string to make a Venn diagram.)
2. One player (the sorter) chooses two cards and places each of the cards, facedown, in the outer circles of the diagram.
3. Other players try to guess what the cards say by taking turns choosing a block and handing it to the sorter.
4. The sorter decides if the block belongs in one of the outer rings, in the center where the rings overlap, or outside the rings altogether.

Look at this example and see if you can determine what the cards say:

In this case, the two cards would have to be "small" and "square." Each player gets only one chance to guess what the cards say. If a player is incorrect, he stops playing until the next round.

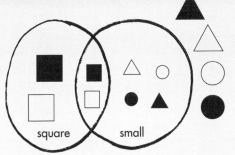

Number Sense

The ability to understand number is measured by questions 1, 2, 4, 5, 14, 17, and 21 on the Math Assessment.

Number sense is knowledge about numbers independent of counting. It is the understanding that 25 would be a reasonable number of raisins to hold in your hand, 235 would not. A living room might be 20 feet long but rarely 80 feet. A gymnasium, on the other hand, would need to be at least 80 feet long. A child who has good number sense can look at the solution to a math problem and know whether or not that number is a reasonable answer.

Children develop number sense by estimating and checking. About how many marbles would fit in this jar? About how much will these three items cost? About how many odd jobs will you need to do before you can buy those items? About how many stars are there in the sky? How can we find out? Numbers such as 100, 1,000, 10,000, and 1,000,000 *slowly* begin to take on greater meaning.

Number sense is also an understanding of mathematical relationships. It is the knowledge that if you multiply numbers (by numbers other than zero or one) you get a greater number. If you divide numbers (by numbers other than zero or one) you get a smaller number. It is the understanding that addition and subtraction are related operations; so are multiplication and division. Multiplication is repeated addition.

Children develop a strong number sense by recognizing visual clusters and patterns. They recognize the pattern of dots on dice or dominoes without counting. They can glance at a pile of books, three red and four blue, and know without counting that there are six in the pile. They can look at a graph, know instantly which group has more or less, and make sound judgments based on the comparisons.

A growing understanding of numbers and patterns allow children to look at the table below and predict what numbers will come next.

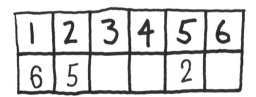

When working with patterns, children begin to make assumptions about larger numbers based on their concrete experiences with smaller ones.

No doubt your third grader will spend more time this year working with symbols (numerals, +, −, >, <, ×, and fractions). In many schools, the amount of time spent working with math manipulatives (blocks, beans, Tangrams, scales) decreases considerably in third grade, while the number of worksheets increases. Although worksheets and workbook pages can provide problems for children to ponder, they are an ineffective means of teaching mathematical concepts. A child who is told how to find a missing addend (11 − __ = 5) by subtracting the smaller number from the larger number has memorized a trick. A trick that will be added to a quickly growing (and often confused or forgotten) list of other tricks. The child who has discovered the relationship between the numbers 5, 6, and 11 by working with objects has acquired a concept that will be retained always.

Is there ever a time when memorization is appropriate? Yes. After a child has developed a true understanding of the quantity of numbers and the way an operation works, then memorizing basic facts makes sense. (What if we had to stop and figure out the spelling of each and every word as we wrote? What a laborious task that would be!) When working on more complex problems, children benefit from quick recall of facts. In the third grade, it is recommended that children memorize their addition and subtraction facts.

As much as you may want to teach your child how to do math, mathematical concepts, unfortunately, cannot be handed down. Children cannot simply be told how numbers work; they must discover that for themselves. However, whether or not your child has the opportunity to develop good number sense, and therefore greater confidence in her math ability, is entirely within your control. With a little awareness and ingenuity, you can provide an environment where curiosity and the desire to learn more about numbers thrives.

THINKING ABOUT LARGE NUMBERS

By now, your child has probably had the opportunity to hear or read David Schwartz's book *How Much Is a Million?* (Morrow), which helps kids to visualize large numbers. Nevertheless, you'll probably want to take it out of the library for another read now and then. The concept of large numbers is one that is acquired *slowly*. Other books to keep an eye out for are *Is a Blue Whale the Biggest Thing There Is?* and *What's Smaller Than a Pigmy Shrew?*, both by Robert E. Wells (Albert Whitman). In these books, Mr. Wells combines knowledge of science, size, and large numbers. If your child shows interest and appreciation for these books, suggest that he write and illustrate his own book about number comparisons.

HAVE FIVE MINUTES?

➤ **Estimate, Check, Revise** Learning to make reasonable estimates takes time and practice. It also should be noted that estimating length, weight, and time is easier for third graders than estimating volume. When estimating, ask your child to give you a guess based on the information available. Then, together, check the estimate. When you've counted or measured halfway, stop and ask your child if he would like to revise his estimate based on what he now knows. For instance, you might ask your child to predict the weight of eight potatoes at the grocer's. After you have placed four in the scale, ask him if he would like to change his prediction. This way, you'll not only have provided practice in estimation—and in thinking about the fraction 1/2—but more important, your child will experience success in coming up with a reasonable estimate. (Remember, estimates are not supposed to be exact. Begin your questions with "About how many . . .") Here are some opportunities for estimating.

- About how many minutes does it take you to eat breakfast each morning?
- About how many spoonfuls of cereal are in your bowl?
- About how many pounds does your backpack weigh before you go to school? When you get home from school?
- About how many steps is it from our door to the bus stop?
- About how long will it take you to walk to the library?
- About how many shoes will fit on the bottom of this closet?
- About how many photographs will fit on this album page?
- About how many Legos (choose one size) can you place around the rim of our bathtub?

➤ If you're out for dinner, ask your child to estimate the costs before the bill comes. If you're at the grocer's, ask your child to estimate the cost of your purchases before you get to the cash register. Encourage your child to count out the exact change. Review coin values if necessary.

➤ **Equations** It doesn't take long for children in the primary grades to translate the equal sign to "the answer is." Break this model and enlarge your child's thinking by challenging him to come up with equations like this: $7 + 5 = 6 + 6$ or $4 + 9 = 15 - 2$. You write the first half of the equation and invite him to write the second. When you get good at this game, see how long you can keep one equation going: $4 + 9 = 15 - 2 = 6 + 7 = 5 + 8 = 14 - 1 = ?$

➤ **What's Missing?** Here's a way to help your child gain more understanding of what happens to numbers when we use the basic operations of addition and subtraction. Present number sentences with blanks where the addition or subtraction signs belong, and have your child determine the missing signs. Allowing your child to use a calculator to try her guesses will enable her to explore more problems and test her thinking with greater ease. Once your child is familiar with multiplication and perhaps division, you can add these signs to your equations.

$$6 \square 2 \square 3 = 5$$
$$9 \square 4 \square 2 \square 8 = 11$$

➤ Some third graders still cringe when they see problems on worksheets that require them to determine the missing addend: $6 + \_\_ = 13$; $\_\_ + 5 = 11$; $16 - \_\_ = 7$. If your child is one of them, spend some time demonstrating this addition and subtraction model:

1. On a sheet of paper, draw a large triangle divided as shown in the figure below.
2. Give your child a group of pennies and ask him to count them. Put the number of the total or the "whole" at the top of the triangle.
3. Now ask him to divide the pennies into two groups (they do not need to be equal). Count the pennies in each group and write the numbers in the spaces below the whole. These numbers represent the parts.
4. With the pennies, ask you child to show you the following examples: Part + Part = __ (Whole); Whole – Part = __ (Other Part); Whole – Other Part = __ (Part); and finally Part + __ (Other Part) = Whole.
5. Give your child a missing addend problem such as $7 + \_\_ = 13$. With the triangle organizer and pennies, have your child show you the missing part.

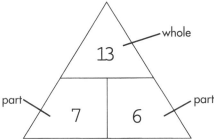

➤ **Talk It Out** Many children simply get tripped up by the symbols in a missing addend problem. Have your child "talk out loud" while thinking about the problem. For instance, he might say: "Thirteen subtract something is nine. So nine plus something is thirteen. Nine plus one is ten. So nine plus four is thirteen and thirteen subtract four is nine."

➤ Does your child have an interest in magic tricks? Many number tricks work not because of the magician's psychic ability but because of a knowledge of basic algebra. Introduce a couple of these tricks to your third grader and suggest he figure out for himself how they work. (He might do so by beginning with different numbers and looking for patterns or by writing equations using n for the missing numbers. What makes these tricks predictable?) You might even encourage him to invent a number trick of his own!

THINK OF A NUMBER
Think of a number from one to ten.
Now double it.
Add six to your new number.
Take half of your answer.
Now subtract your answer from the original number.
Your answer is three.

PHONE BOOK PHONY
Call a friend and tell him to pick a number from one to ten.
Add a zero to the end. (If the friend picked 6 the number would be 60.)
Reverse that number and subtract it from the number before.
    $(60 - 06 = 54)$
Reverse that answer and add it to the number that came before.
    $(45 + 54 = 99)$
Now take the last number and turn to that page in your phone book.
    Count 9 names down from the top.
I bet that name is (read the name from your matching phone book.)

➤ Does your third grader have a birthday coming up? Look for Hocus Pocus Junior magic kits by Jumbo International. Their "presentation kits" provide several number games—no sleight-of-hand required. Again, challenge your child to figure out how these games work.

➤ **Memorizing Math Facts** As mentioned, this is the year your child should memorize his addition and subtraction facts to eighteen if he hasn't done so already. Hopefully, he has had plenty of practice in using concrete materials and real-life problems to develop a sense of numbers and strategies for adding or subtracting mentally. However, even the best strategies will slow him down in later problem solving if he has to stop and calculate what $7 + 8$ is every time he comes to it. There are many fun ways to help your child memorize these facts. Please note that a couple of these activities suggest timing your child. Some children love being clocked and strive to beat their own time. Other children hate it and actually make more mistakes when under time-pressure. There is no reason to time children other than to make the activity of memorizing facts more interesting. Make sure you choose the activities that will build your child's confidence rather than break it down.

- Suggest that your child create rhymes or jingles to remember more difficult math facts:

  "What's six plus seven?" said the queen. Don't you know that it's thirteen?

  Some children simply have more success memorizing their math facts when music plays in the background.

- Have your child add spaghetti to vinegar. Suggest he count the number of letters in each word and add the numbers together. Encourage him to come up with his own combinations to add or subtract. How many different word combinations can he find for each fact?

  spaghetti = 9

  vinegar = 7

  9 + 7 = 16

- Suggest that your child write his nines addition facts and look for patterns. Can he see a way to add numbers to nine more quickly?

- Do you have a Twister game mat? Have your child begin on a dot in the lower right corner. Hold up flashcards (have him make them following the directions below) and encourage him to call out the answers as quickly as he can. Each time he answers correctly, have him move to the next dot (down one row of colored dots and then up the next row). Time how quickly he can reach the last one. Then encourage him to try to beat his time. If he had repeated trouble with one of the facts, have him repeat the fact family (7 + 8 = 15, 8 + 7 = 15, 15 − 8 = 7, 15 − 7 = 8) a few times before beginning again.

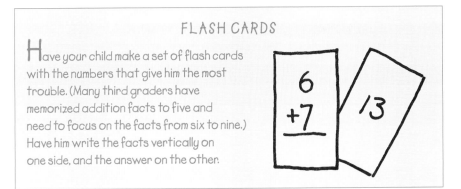

FLASH CARDS

Have your child make a set of flash cards with the numbers that give him the most trouble. (Many third graders have memorized addition facts to five and need to focus on the facts from six to nine.) Have him write the facts vertically on one side, and the answer on the other.

• Play Add! with your child. This game is similar to the card game War, but instead of the player with the larger number getting the cards, the first person to add the two numbers flipped from the top of the piles takes them all. (Treat jacks, queens, and kings as 0.) If you're up on your addition facts, you might give your child a 5-count lead each time. Once he has memorized his facts, you can race to shout the answer. You can also play Subtract! by subtracting the smaller number from the larger.

HAVE MORE TIME?

➤ Play dominoes and dice games with your third grader. Look for this title from Planet Dexter: *Shake, Rattle, and Roll! Cool Things to Do with Dice (that grown ups don't even know about).*

➤ **Board Games** When was the last time you played a board game with your third grader? If you haven't done so recently, dust off the covers of one of your old favorites and prepare for some real competition. You may have let your child win a few rounds of Candy Land when he was younger, but that's a thing of the past. Games for older children require logic and strategic thinking in addition to chance, and after a few practice games you'll find that your third grader is up to the task. In addition to the fun you'll have together, you'll help him develop concepts and critical thinking skills essential for mathematical understanding. If you choose only one activity from "Number Sense," choose to play one of these games:

battleship	Chinese checkers
card games	mancala
(gin rummy, poker, hearts, blackjack—	parcheesi
or teach your child solitaire)	tangrams
checkers	Uno
chess	Yahtzee

Place Value with Addition and Subtraction

The ability to comprehend concept of place value and to work with larger numbers in addition and subtraction is measured by questions 1, 2, 3, and 14 on the Math Assessment.

By now your child has probably been exposed to and can, with some sophistication, talk about place value. She may be able to identify the hundreds, tens, and ones column in a three-digit number. She may be able to add with regrouping (carrying) and subtract with renaming (borrowing). She may even be able to do mental arithmetic with large numbers—adding the tens first and later adding the ones to total. But this does not mean that your third grader shouldn't spend many more hours exploring our base-ten system.

Place value is often to primary school children what counting is to the toddler. A toddler sounds very bright and mathematically inclined when counting to thirteen. Many a proud parent comes to the conclusion that the toddler knows about numbers, that he realizes that one number represents one object. But this is not usually the case. In both instances—the case of the precocious toddler, and the third grader who adds three-digit numbers with ease—the language of math has preceded a thorough understanding of the concepts.

It is not often apparent to teachers, parents, or the child that the base-ten system is not fully understood until the student needs to apply the information to later learning. Multiplication, division, and particularly the decimal system, all require a solid understanding of place value. A child who has simply memorized processes such as carrying and borrowing will find that learning the tricks becomes more and more difficult. Confusion sets in. So does math anxiety. The child who once breezed through math suddenly finds that it just doesn't make sense anymore.

Ask your child to take you through the steps of adding or subtracting larger numbers (or column addition). Ask questions as she goes along. Why are you beginning with the numbers on the right side? How come you put a one here? How do you know that your answer is a reasonable one? Or explore your child's understanding of place value. Can you show me *another* way of adding these numbers together? For instance, a child who truly understands place value might suggest solving the problem $37 + 48$ by adding the tens first in this way:

$30 + 40 = 70$
$7 + 8 = 15$
$70 + 15 = 85$
or she might come up with this solution by rounding and subtracting:
37 rounds to $40 (-3)$
48 rounds to $50 (-2)$
$40 + 50 = 90$
$3 + 2 = 5$
$90 - 5 = 85$

If you focus on just one area of math at home, place value would be a fine choice. By playing games and exploring patterns in the base-ten system, you would be assuring that those small roots—the foundation of further math development—grow deep and spread far.

➤ Play Roll Out a Number—another activity for two. Although it is relevant for your third grader, a younger child or an older child will also love the element of chance in this game.

ROLL OUT A NUMBER

1. Have each player create a game board that has blank spaces for ten three-digit numbers.
2. Take turns rolling the die three times for each round. After each roll, players decide whether to place the number in the hundreds, tens, or ones column.
3. Player with the highest three-digit number gets a point for each round. Both players get a point on a tie.
4. The player with the most number of points when the boards are filled wins.
5. After your children have worn this game out, have them attempt to record the lowest number on each round.

➤ Now try HiLo.

1. Each player draws an addition diagram like this:

2. Players take turns rolling the die and choosing a position in the diagram for that number.
3. When the diagrams are filled, players add their numbers. The player with the highest (or lowest, depending on which way you want to play) wins.

➤ Play One Hundred. Take two egg cartons and cut off the last two cups on each. Now pour a bowl of macaroni, buttons, or pennies—you will need approximately two hundred small objects. Each player takes turns rolling a die and placing the appropriate number of objects in the first egg cup. No egg cup may have more than ten objects, and each egg cup must be completely filled before a player starts to fill another. The first player to reach one hundred objects wins.

➤ **Calculator Fun** Remember a time when you didn't go anywhere without crayons in your pocket or your purse? You knew that in a pinch, you had an instant activity. Well, now that your child is an eager third grader, you might want to consider carrying a pocket calculator to create impromptu moments for learning. Here is one place value game for your calculator.

- Type in a four-digit number such as 3,456
- Have your child erase the number in four sequential steps (thousands place to ones place): 3,000, 400, 50, 6
- If he makes a mistake, have him start over.
- When your child becomes adept at erasing four-digit numbers, go to five- and six-digit numbers.

➤ Draw a diagram like the one below. Using numbers one to nine only once (you may carry a number used) complete the addition problem so that it is true. There are more than a hundred ways to solve this problem.

➤ Teach your child the game 500. Take turns rolling dice, using the two numerals to make the largest number you can and subtracting it from 500. The first player to get to zero wins. If you roll a one, you have to add the numbers instead of subtracting. If either of you roll two ones, you're back to 500.

➤ Got a sports fan? Calculate statistics while reading the newspaper or watching an event on television together: If this team has won seventeen games this season, how many have they lost? What is the combined weight of the defensive line? You may also want to search for these books, which would inspire a multitude of problems to solve: *Sports Facts; Pocket Full of Knowledge* by Norman Barrett (Dorling Kindersley) and *Everything You Want to Know About Sports Encyclopedia* by Neil Cohen (Sports Illustrated Kids).

➤ Give your child real problems to solve. Encourage her to develop her own system for finding answers. She may come up with a process that differs from the one you or she has been taught. But if she does, chances are she will be developing a more accurate understanding of numbers. Here are some examples of problems you might present:

- When we woke up this morning, the temperature was 37 degrees. Now it is 14 degrees! How many degrees has the temperature fallen?
- What is our family's combined bowling score? (weight, ages)
- I have to cook the potatoes for 90 minutes and the rolls for an added 25. How many minutes until dinner?
- Here are the prices for the separate party goods and favors. What is the total price? What would the price be if we didn't buy paper plates?
- We need to travel from here to Aunt Jane's, 69 miles away. Then we'll go on to Grandpa's house, which is 45 miles from Aunt Jane's. How many miles will we travel today?

HAVE MORE TIME?

➤ Play Monopoly. Exchanging money in denominations of ones, tens, and hundred-dollar bills provides wonderful practice in learning about place value.

Multiplication

The ability to multiply whole numbers is measured by questions 14, 17, 18, and 20 on the Math Assessment.

First grade babies, second grade bums, third grade angels, fourth grade sugar plums.

Third grade. The year a child graduates to angel. The year a child learns cursive writing. The year a child learns multiplication! Sure, second grade has carrying and borrowing, and fifth grade has decimals. But children seldom pine for that specific knowledge in the same way they do for the wisdom of multiplication.

Memorizing multiplication tables has become part of our cultural lore, a rite of passage. Parents have lived to tell about the ordeal, children's books and TV shows present characters facing the "times tables" as the ultimate challenge. Like learning to skip count (reciting multiples), children discover that multiplying gets them working with those dazzling big numbers. (Kids remember that $12 \times 12 = 144$ long before they know the answer to 6×7.) Most third graders can't wait to test their mettle.

Because your child is so motivated, and because you remember how *you* learned multiplication, you may be tempted to get right down to the business of reciting and memorizing multiplication facts. There is nothing wrong with memorization. At some point children need to have memorized the facts in order to solve problems efficiently. (In fact, you may recall a number of strategies presented in "Number Sense" [page 140] to help your child retain addition and subtraction facts.) However, like all math learning, working with symbols should not precede working with concrete materials and real-life problems in order to truly understand the concept and purpose of multiplication.

Tell your child that "multiplication is repeated addition" and his eyes may glaze over. But have him group pennies into five groups of ten for bank rolling, or have him figure out how many touchdowns plus extra points (multiples of seven) are needed for a football team to take the lead, and you will help him discover the beauty of multiplication. In other words, do not introduce your child to multiplication by simply giving him a series of facts to retain; instead, provide him with opportunities to build on what he already knows.

In most schools, students are expected to have memorized their multiplication facts by the end of third grade. In other schools, students are not expected to have learned the facts cold until fourth grade. Either way, keep in mind that if you help your child memorize multiplication facts, you will have taught him to respond quickly. But teach your child how and *when* to multiply in addition to memorizing and you will have taught him how to think mathematically. Here are some suggestions for doing both.

HAVE FIVE MINUTES?

➤ While at the dinner table or driving in the car, talk about things that come in twos (eyes, bicycle tires, socks), threes (stop lights, cupcakes, tricycle wheels), fours (car wheels, cat legs, corners on a sandbox), fives (fingers, car tires if you count the spare), and sixes (six pack of soda, half dozen eggs, sides on a die). After you've explored these numbers at length, pose word problems: If you had four cars, how many wheels would you have in all?

➤ While waiting for a pot to boil or the laundry to dry, give your child a sheet of paper and a pencil and ask her to draw four cats. Then say, "Give each of your cats a hat. How many hats is that? Place two birds on each hat. How many birds are there in all? Give each cat three bells. How many bells are there in all? Give each cat four sneakers. How many sneakers is that?" Go for as long as your child is having fun. Some children will guess the sequence and want to come up with what to draw next. Encourage this participation.

➤ While shopping, look at products that are sold in groups. "Look, juice boxes come in packages of three. How many boxes will we have if I buy three packages?" Or, "These pastries cost fifty cents apiece. How many will four cost?"

➤ Have a collector? Chances are his collection will provide lots of opportunities for multiplying. If you place three baseball cards on each page of this album, how many cards will six pages hold? If you put two bean bag animals in each shoe pocket, and there are eight pockets, how many animals will this shoe bag hold?"

➤ Teach your child how to skip-count by threes and fours. You might begin by recalling how your child learned to count by twos. Did he do it by memorizing a rhyme such as "Two, four, six, eight. Who do we appreciate?" If so, invent a rhyme for threes. "Three, six, nine, twelve. Fifteen, eighteen on the shelves." Perhaps he learned simply by thinking ahead one. If so, you might want to draw a number line to help him visualize counting ahead by threes or fours.

➤ **Lattice Model** Once your child has demonstrated an understanding of multiplication while using concrete objects, you might want to introduce a lattice model. Show your child how to set up a multiplication problem by drawing horizontal lines to represent one number and vertical lines to represent the other. Help him find and count the dots where the lines cross. For instance, the problem 4×6 would look like this.

Or it could look like this:

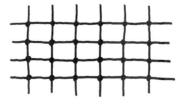

The beauty of this model is it helps children to recognize the commutative property of multiplication ($4 \times 6 = 24$, $6 \times 4 = 24$).

➤**Tile Model** Another way to reinforce the concept of multiplication is to go to your local tile store and ask for extras or toss-aways of their smallest tiles (most stores have samples or incomplete sheets that they don't mind parting with if you let them know you'll be using them to help teach your child math). Or, if you have a Scrabble game, have your child use the letter tiles for this activity. Demonstrate how to use the tiles to create rectangles. Begin by asking: Can you make a rectangle that is two tiles by two tiles? Five tiles by two tiles? What would a rectangle that is two tiles by five tiles look like? Give your child multiplication problems and have him solve them by creating rectangles. This model is useful for helping your child visualize problems that use larger numbers.

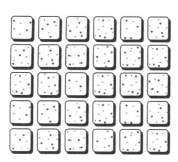

$6 \times 5 = 30$

➤Don't have time to visit a tile store? You can show your child the rectangle model by using graph paper. Have him color in boxes to create rectangles that represent particular multiplication problems.

➤**Nines Trick** So when *is* it okay to introduce math shortcuts? After your child has demonstrated a thorough knowledge of how a math process works, then it's appropriate to introduce a speedier trick. For instance, when your child has spent a good deal of time working with concrete objects, can articulate an understanding of multiplication, and is ready to begin memorizing facts, show him the nines trick. One simple way of determining multiples of nine is to use one's fingers. Hold up your hands. The pinkie on your left hand is one. To multiply 3 times 9, you would put down finger number 3. The fingers to the left of the missing finger are tens, the fingers to the right are ones. Therefore, the answer to 3 times 9 is 27.

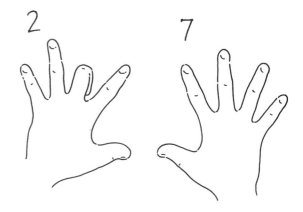

➤ Here's one more nines trick—one that doesn't involve fingers. Have your child pick a nines fact such as 9×7. Tell him to subtract one from the 7 (6). Now ask, 6 plus what number equals 9? (3) The answer is 63. This system works for 1×9 to 10×9.

➤ You can use many of the suggestions for memorizing math facts provided on page 144 to help your child memorize multiplication tables. In addition, you might want to invite your child to make up "rap songs" to memorize rhymes. Here's a rap from Gina Willner-Pardo's *Spider Storch's Teacher Torture* (Albert Whitman):

> Eight times four equals thirty-two.
> You hear what I'm sayin', 'cause I'm telling you.
> Eight times five equals forty, I say.
> It will tomorrow and it does today.

HAVE MORE TIME?

➤ Give your child a blank multiplication grid from page 221. Show him how to use his fingers to find the coordinate points. For instance, show him how to place one finger on the two at the top of the table, another finger on the two on the side of the table and then to follow the boxes until his fingers meet. Encourage him to write the answer to 2×2 in this empty box. Suggest that he begin completing the table by filling in his two facts. Then ask, What other facts are easy for you? Certainly one facts are easy. So are fives and tens. What other multiples are easy? If your child has been skip-counting by threes and fours, then those facts will be easy to complete. If your child is a football fan, the sevens facts will come rather easily. By now, your child's grid might look something like this:

1	2	3	4	5	6	7	8	9	10
2	4	6	8	10	12	14	16	18	20
3	6	9	12	15	18	21	24	27	30
4	8	12				28			40
5	10	15	20	25	30	35	40	45	50
6	12	18				42			60
7	14	21				49			70
8	16	24				56			80
9	18	27				63			90
10	20	30	40	50	60	70	80	90	100

Say, "Look! You have so few multiplication facts to memorize!" If your child hasn't learned the "nines trick" now would be a fine time to introduce it (see above). Also, have your child use his own method to figure out the eleven table. He'll see a pattern before no time.

➤ Using tiles or graph paper, show your child how to break a difficult multiplication problem, such as 7×8, down to simpler problems to solve. Here's how:
  1. Have your child make a rectangle that represents 7×8.
  2. Ask your child which multiples he finds easier than sevens. If he suggests twos, have him make a rectangle that is 2×8.
  3. Point out that 5 plus 2 equals 7. Have him make a rectangle to show 5×8.
  4. Now have him place the smaller rectangles over the large one. (If he is using graph paper he can cut the rectangles out to do this.)
  5. Guide him to understand that the problem 7×8 could be done this way: $2 \times 8 = 16, 5 \times 8 = 40. 40 + 16 = 56$.

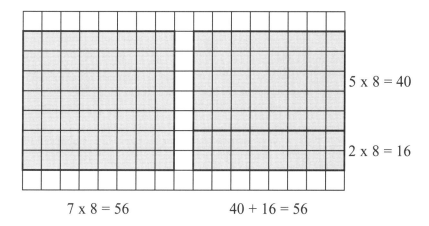

5 x 8 = 40

2 x 8 = 16

7 x 8 = 56   40 + 16 = 56

➤ **Two-Digit Multiplication** Show your child how to multiply a two-digit number by a single number (13×5). In doing so, refrain from teaching your child an algorithm (procedure) in which you "carry a one." (Which of course, is really a ten.) Most children in third grade haven't had enough experience with place value or multiplication to understand how that procedure would work. Instead, teach your child to multiply the 5 by the number of tens ($10 \times 5 = 50$), then ones ($3 \times 5 = 15$) and then add the products together: $50 + 15 = 65$. Better yet, before introducing any procedure, have your child try to come up with her own. This way you can determine what she understands before guiding her in a new direction.

Measurement

The ability to use measurement to solve problems is assessed by questions 6, 7, 8, 9, 10, 11, 12, and 13 on the Math Assessment.

Hopefully, your third grader has had practice in measuring length and width using nonstandard units of measurement (blocks, paper clips, strides) and standard units of measurement (U.S. customary and metric rulers). She has likely been exposed to balance scales, measuring cups, and thermometers. Perhaps she has learned that string makes a handy tool for measuring round things and that cups of rice or beans can help one compare capacity. In other words, she has been exposed to various measuring tools and how to use them.

In addition to learning new ways to measure (area, perimeter, capacity, elapsed and calendar time), this year your child will be given opportunities to extend her understanding of measurement concepts. Grappling with more sophisticated ideas about measurement will help her to develop greater muscle and flexibility when problem solving. The activities that support this growth are divided into two sections: measurement practice and measurement concepts.

Measurement Practice

Along with plenty of continued practice in standard linear measurement (centimeters, meters, inches, feet, yards), your child should be introduced to the measurement of area, perimeter, liquid capacity, and elapsed time this year. He should be able to tell time to the minute and grow in his knowledge of calendar time. Here are some specific terms and information to introduce:

Area is the amount of surface inside a figure. Introduce this topic with your dining room table: About how many index cards (chapter books, jar lids, placemats) can you fit on the table top? Then respond using the measurement unit in your answer, "Oh, our table top has an area of about 113 index cards!"

Perimeter is the distance around the edge or rim of a figure. You can help your child remember this definition by recalling that the word "perimeter" contains the word "rim." Have your child measure the rim of the table top (length + length + width + width) using the same nonstandard unit he used to measure the area.

Elapsed time is the duration of time passed. The elapsed time between 2:00 and 4:30 is 2 1/2 hours. The best way to introduce the concept of elapsed time is to ask your third grader questions about her day: How long was math class today? How long did it take you to complete your spelling homework? How many times can you sing "Row Row Row Your Boat" in one minute?

Calendar time is an understanding of how our system of time is structured. Help your third grader to remember that there are 60 seconds in a minute, 60 minutes in an hour, 24 hours in a day, 365 days in a year. He should also realize that, with the exception of February, months have 30 or 31 days, and that there are 52 weeks in a year. Give your child plenty of opportunity to observe and explore these numbers by attaching them to real experiences.

Capacity is the amount a container will hold. By providing experience in the kitchen and at market you can help your third grader learn that there are 2 cups in a pint, 2 pints in a quart, and 4 quarts in a gallon. He will also need to know that a teaspoon holds about 5 milliliters, and a liter holds 1,000 milliliters, which is just under a quart of milk.

HAVE FIVE MINUTES?

➤ Keep a variety of measuring tools around your home. Rulers, tape measures, string, scoops, measuring cups, measuring spoons, and thermometers will provide opportunities to answer unexpected questions: "I thought photographs and index cards were both 3×5, how come these look bigger? How come the ice cream in the freezer is soft? Which creates more liquid when melted, a scoop of ice cream or an ice cube?" Having measuring tools handy encourages experimentation and keeps those questions coming.

➤ Help your child establish her own points of reference when using linear measurement. Provide her with a ruler and ask, "Can you find something on your hand that is about one inch (centimeter) long?" She may discover that the distance from the knuckle to the tip of her thumb is an inch, the fingernail on her pinkie is approximately a centimeter. Being able to visualize a measurement unit in this way will help her to estimate length in the future.

➤ You can use this same technique for helping your third grader imagine longer distances. While driving to a familiar place, clock one mile on your car's odometer. Now she can recall that one mile is "from our house to the Laundromat." Or if she walks to school, you might use a pedometer to measure the distance. Knowing that the walk is half a mile will help her estimate other distances in the future.

➤ Study a ruler with your child. Make sure she knows that a ruler is 12 inches. Then ask her to predict whether objects around the house are more or less than a foot. Have her measure to check her guesses.

➤ Third graders may look like big kids, but they still love to pour. Challenging your child to discover how many medicine spoons (10 milliliters) of water it takes to fill your coffeepot (one liter) will have her putting her hands into water instantly. Come to think of it, having her compare the capacity of measuring spoons, cups, bowls, shampoo containers, and milk jugs just might get all the dishes washed, and the recycles rinsed!

➤ Explore area by using small tiles (from a local tile store or Scrabble game tiles) or draw figures on graph paper. Begin with a rectangle:

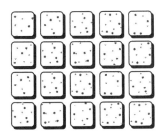

Ask, "How many squares are on the surface of the rectangle? Right, this rectangle has an area of 20 squares." As your child is exposed to concepts of multiplication, she may realize that the area of a rectangle can be determined by multiplying 5×4. This is a terrific discovery, but try not to show her yourself. Instead, give her lots of practice in finding the area of rectangles and see if she can't make the connection. We are far more likely to retain a formula if we discover it on our own.

➤ Using tiles or graph paper, challenge your third grader to create as many different shapes as possible with the same perimeter. Have him measure the perimeter by counting the sides of each tile or square on the outer rim. How many shapes can he come up with? Or play a game in which one of you draws a shape, and the other has to draw a different shape with the same perimeter. Then switch roles.

➤ **Area and Perimeter** Ask your child to explore the question: Do figures that have the same perimeter have the same area? Encourage him to explore the answer in his own way. Once he has discovered the answer, ask, "Do different figures with the same area have the same perimeter?" Again, let him explore. Once your child has reached the conclusion that *no* is the answer to both questions, ask, "How can this be?" Have him share his experiments and give you his reasoning.

➤ Developing a good sense of time can take a lifetime. Try this experiment with your family and friends. Designate one person to be the timer. Provide him with a stopwatch or a watch with a second hand and a list of the other people present. Then ask everyone else to close their eyes and silently raise their hands when they think a minute has passed. Have someone record the seconds elapsed when each hand is raised next to the appropriate player's name. Do not stop timing or say anything aloud until the last hand is raised. You'll be amazed with the discrepancies in time! If you wish, repeat the experiment and have players raise their hands when three minutes have passed.

➤ Buy a stopwatch. Young children, especially third graders, adore stopwatches. Your child will spend endless hours, minutes, and seconds recording everything from how long it takes his brother to brush his teeth to how long it takes you to whistle "Yankee Doodle." Needless to say, this is a great way for him to grow in his understanding of elapsed time. If you're looking for a future gift, you might want to keep an eye out for *Stop! The Watch: A Book of Everyday, Ordinary Olympics* (Klutz Press), which comes with a stopwatch.

➤ Include time in your response to your third grader's requests. It might seem odd to you both at first to say, "You can have a snack at 3:13," or "Yes, let's go to the library at 4:57," but it sure will help him to tell time to the minute!

➤ Don't stop asking your child for the time. After he has responded, ask, "What time will it be in 12 minutes? What time was it 19 minutes ago?"

➤ Give your third grader plenty of opportunities to compare Fahrenheit and Celsius temperatures. What is the freezing point on each of these scales? What are the boiling points? Tell him the temperature before going out in the morning and have him guess whether you are giving Fahrenheit or Celsius degrees.

HAVE MORE TIME?

➤ Plan a project together. Whenever you cook, sew, do carpentry, or set up an impromptu soccer game, you use measuring skills. While working together, encourage your third grader to identify what needs to be measured, how to measure it, and how accurate the measurement needs to be. Help your child to see that moving a piece of furniture from one wall

MEASUREMENT
PROJECTS

Here are some project ideas that involve measuring skills:

BUILD
A bird house
An elf village
A doll house
A fort

SEW
Bean bag animals
Cloth bags
A family banner
A costume

COOK
Homemade clay
A batch of brownies
A celebration dinner
A meal for the homeless

to another, a pinch of salt, and the length of the neighborhood playing field require approximate measures. But that measuring the width of each drawer to make a dresser, the amount of liquid in a recipe, or the width of a soccer goal in a tournament require more precise measurements. Discuss what would happen if the latter measurements were not accurate. You might want to introduce your child to the expression: "Measure twice, cut once," if you haven't already.

➤ Create a treasure hunt to help your third grader practice measuring. You might provide a series of clues such as: *The next clue you'll see is three yards from the tree. But what direction should you go? Find a root twenty-eight inches long and you'll know.* Or draw a treasure map and include a scale to indicate accurate distances between landmarks. When your third grader begs you to do it again, suggest that she create the hunt or treasure map for you to follow.

➤ Suggest that she make her own calendar. Make twelve photocopies of the Calendar Page on page 222. Using a commercial calendar as a guide, have her write in the correct numbers and illustrate the top of each page if she wishes. Next, suggest she record important dates—holidays, birthdays, events to look forward to. Help her to hang the calendar in a prominent place and refer to it often.

Measurement Concepts

Third graders are intellectually ready to grasp the following concepts:

1. Objects can be measured in different ways for different purposes. For instance, we measure the length and width of a tent to determine how many sleepers it will hold, and we measure the weight of a tent to determine whether it's appropriate for backpacking.
2. One chooses a measuring tool depending on the size of the object to be measured and the purpose of the measurement. A six-inch ruler is wonderful for measuring the growth of a seedling, but inadequate for measuring the length of a fence.
3. All measurement is approximate (subject to the tools and the user) and often approximate measurements (it's about four feet) are sufficient.

The activities listed below will give your third grader plenty of practice in working with these concepts.

HAVE FIVE MINUTES?

➤ Help your child apply his growing knowledge of area and perimeter to new concepts. Suggest he trace his hand on a sheet of paper. Ask him which would take more beans: the area or the perimeter of his hand. Remind him that the area is the space inside his tracing, the perimeter is the line around his hand. After he has made an estimate, give him a few handfuls of dried beans and have him measure.

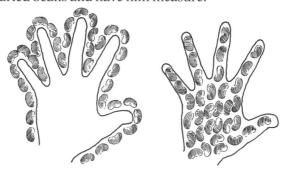

Then ask if these measurements are exact. Help him to see that they are not because (1) the beans are not all the same size, (2) some white space still surrounds the beans, and (3) the line of his hand might be different each time it is traced. Nevertheless, this inexact measurement gives us the information we need: Which is larger, the area or the perimeter?

➤ Repeat the exercise above by having him trace the bottom of his shoe. After he has estimated and checked his response, extend his thinking with more questions: When do you think we might need to know the area of an object? When do you think we might need to know the perimeter?

➤ The next time you fold laundry, ask your child, "Can you put the piles in order according to size?" There are many valid ways that she could solve this problem. She could
- count the number of items in each pile
- measure or "eye" the height of each pile
- use a scale to compare the weight of each pile
- compare the area of the top item in each pile

   Praise her approach and then ask, "Can you measure the piles in another way?" See how many solutions she comes up with on her own. Children's thinking is often ingenious, she may come up with a way that is not mentioned here.

➤ For a more difficult challenge, give her four boxes of differing sizes and shapes—a cereal box, a square gift box, a pizza box, and a shoe box. Ask your third grader to put these boxes in the order of size. When she has figured out one way to solve the problem, ask her to tell you how she did it.

Then ask, "Do you think there's another way?" Or, "How could you measure how much each box holds?"

➤ Next time you're driving in the car, or waiting for the subway together, ask your child to consider open-ended measurement questions. (As you've seen, there are many correct answers to these questions.) What would you use to measure

the width of a piece of paper?

the bottom of a cup?

the capacity of a bottle?

the length of a sidewalk?

the area of a rug?

the perimeter of a garden?

If she chooses a method that may be time consuming (measuring the length of a sidewalk with a ruler), ask, "Can you think of a faster way?"

➤ Find an assortment of random objects and pose this problem: Can you find the weight of these items without putting them directly on the scale?

HAVE MORE TIME?

➤ Got a long rainy day ahead of you? Suggest that your child measure the length of the room using: shoes, flyswatters (show her how to mark the end of each unit with her finger or a piece of tape, so she can lift the flyswatter over and over), dog biscuits, bean bag animals—anything you or she can think of. Have her record her results on a bar graph (for more information on making bar graphs, see "Probability and Statistics," page 172). When she has completed her research, ask her which unit was the easiest to measure with, which was the most difficult, and why she has drawn these conclusions. Ask, "Do you think you would get the same results if you tried this activity again?"

➤ Using the calendar your child made, or a commercial calendar, invite your third grader to explore the following questions:

• Do some days occur more times in the year than others? Which ones? Why do you think this is so?

• Make a list of Sunday dates, Wednesday dates, and Friday dates. What patterns do you see?

• Do all months have the same number of weeks?

• Look for dates in different months that fall on the same day of the week. Are these months similar in other ways?

Fractions

The ability to work with fractions is measured by questions 8 and 16 on the Math Assessment.

What? My child is only in the third grade. Certainly he doesn't need to be working with fractions yet!

Traditionally, working with fractions was seen as an upper-elementary grade skill—a subject too complex for primary school children to learn. At the most, third graders were introduced to symbolic representations of fractions. They received worksheets with rectangles and circles in which they demonstrated, in fraction notation, which part of the shape was shaded. Sometimes, they were asked to determine the fraction of a set: How many of the children are wearing hats?

Children spent a week or so completing variations of these worksheets and hopefully learned something about equal parts, numerators, and denominators. It is likely that they retained (although perhaps only briefly) a knowledge of two new rules: To find the bottom number of a fraction, you count the number of parts. To find the top number of a fraction, you count the number of shapes shaded. But what could they tell you about fractions aside from how to complete the worksheet?

Not much. Fractions are complex and they require at least as much concrete experience and real-life problem solving as is required to obtain an understanding of whole numbers. (If you read "Number Sense" [page 140] you already know that acquiring knowledge of our number system is far more difficult than it first appears.) We learn to count whole numbers in sequence. We know that with integers, six follows five and seven follows six. We know that six represents a larger quantity than five. Fractions are slipperier. Between two fractions is another fraction. And between those three fractions are many more. And 1/4 is smaller than 1/3, even though everyone knows that four is larger than three.

Thanks in part to the new standards published by the National Council of Teachers of Mathematics (and currently under revision again), math curricula are undergoing positive change. Teachers are now using the knowledge children have acquired about fractions (most third graders have had experience with halves and quarters while sharing food and toys or telling time) and patiently building upon it. They are providing problem-solving activities that allow children to explore and develop a more thorough and enlightened knowledge of this subject. Instead of counting shaded parts of a circle, a third grader is likely to be presented with a problem such as this one: Using colored tiles, build a rectangle that is 1/6 blue, 1/6 green, 1/3 yellow, and 1/3 red. Here are two solutions:

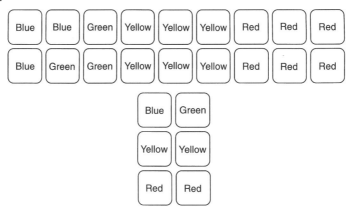

Even so, there are not enough hours or personal attention in the school day to give your child the amount of practice he needs with fractions. This is where you, the parent, can have a profound effect on your child's mathematical understanding and performance. Don't worry if you don't remember the rules of fractions. (How do you find the common denominator? When do you flip the fraction over?) It's not productive, especially at this stage of your child's learning, to pass these shortcuts on. Instead, begin to incorporate "fraction think" into every aspect of your day.

Out of practice? That's okay. You and your third grader can discover and play with fractions together. With a little open-mindedness, flexibility, and persistence, you and your third grader will begin to get a grasp on these numbers as a team. You will come to realize that you don't have to have all the answers, and that the search for a solution is more fun anyway. When you are learning alongside your child, you bring an energy and enthusiasm that isn't always present when reviewing familiar subjects. Try some of these activities and before long you will be recognizing and making sense of fractions everywhere!

➤ When introducing fractions, start with your own family. At the dinner table, ask questions: How many people like spinach? How many like milk? How many went to school today? How many will help with the dishes? Have your third grader (and other eager participants) answer in fractions. For instance, if there are four people in your family, the answer to how many people like spinach might be 2/4.

> FRACTION TALK
>
> Try to incorporate the language of fractions into your normal speaking as often as possible. Discuss your day in fractions: "I spent two thirds of my day at work. Boy, it's good to be spending my last third at home." At meal time, divide food into equal portions and tell the fraction of the portion as you dole it out. It won't be long before your third grader is shouting, "Hey, you gave him three eighths and I only got two eighths!"

➤ It seems as if most children have an easier time with math concepts when it involves money. You might consider structuring your child's weekly or monthly allowance so he has the opportunity to work with fractions. For example, you might give him an amount with the expectation that one third will go toward saving, one third toward giving (church, youth group), and one third toward spending. Another system might require your child to save one quarter, spend one quarter, and pay for school lunches with half. Only you and your child can come up with the system that works best for your family.

➤ **Money Sense** Use coins to represent parts of a whole. Ask, Why do you think a quarter is called a quarter? (Because this coin equals one quarter or 1/4 of a dollar.) What then does a dime equal? (1/10) How about a nickel and a penny? (1/20, 1/100) Can you write a fraction for three nickels? (3/20) How about five nickels? (5/20) With a little practice, you may be able to guide your child into understanding that 1/4 and 5/20 are equal fractions. So are 1/2, 2/4, 10/20, and 50/100!

HAVE MORE TIME?

➤ Hold a sheet of paper horizontally and draw a number line from 0 to 5 across the paper. Now, using clay or Play-Doh, have your child make many snakes of equal length. Divide the first snake in half. Ask your child, "Where would half a snake fall on the number line?" Help her to see that it should be placed halfway between the 0 and the 1. Now have her divide another snake in three equal pieces. Where would one-third fall on the number line? (Between the 0 and 1/2.) Pinch the other two parts back together. Where would two-thirds fall on the line? Experiment in this way, writing the fractions on the line as you go. After a few tries, suggest that your child come up with new ways to divide snakes evenly. Ask her to tell you about the patterns she sees on the number line.

➤ At a later date, add to your number line. This time, use real or clay cookies to make fractions. Where would 1 1/2 fall on your line? 3 2/3? 5 1/8?

➤ If you can, invest in a set of pattern blocks. Sets of plastic or wooden pattern blocks are available in most toy stores and through catalogs. You can also use the pattern block template on page 220 to make your own set out of poster board. You will need at least ten of each shape (twenty-five is even better). Each shape should be a different color so that you can talk about the blocks by color. Chances are you will be amazed at the elaborate designs your child is able to make with these blocks. As she explores, you can ask questions such as:

- Which block is 1/2 the size of the blue diamond?
- How many reds will cover one yellow block? So one red covers how much of the yellow?
- Can you make a design that is half blue and half red?

Geometry

Your child's understanding of geometry is assessed by questions 15 and 16 on the Math Assessment.

Quadrilaterals, pentagons, hexagons, parallelograms, acute angles, obtuse angles. We tend to think of the study of geometry as a highly specialized subject with a code of its own. Geometry can be interesting, maybe even fascinating, but it has little to do with the use of math in everyday life. Right?

Think for a moment. When was the last time you parked your car? Moved a piece of furniture? Gave directions? All of these require spatial thinking—the bedrock of geometry. Engineers, architects, graphic designers, and air traffic controllers are some professions that require knowledge of geometry. But so do artists, carpenters, plumbers, surgeons, mechanics, even football players. Geometry is the study of the spatial world. The ideas of geometry are used to describe, interpret, and change the physical world in which we live.

Rather than being an isolated body of knowledge, geometry impacts every strand of mathematical learning. The ability to sort, classify, recognize patterns, develop measurement formulas, and use deductive reasoning are taught through the discipline of geometry. Children who develop strong spatial skills have a giant advantage in problem solving. This is why it is so important for girls, as well as boys, to play with blocks and interlocking construction toys.

At the third grade level, children learn to:
1. Classify two- and three-dimensional shapes and figures using the properties of edges, corners, and faces.
2. Recognize and name polygons, quadrilaterals, pentagons, hexagons, octagons, cones, cubes, cylinders, prisms, and spheres.
3. Experiment with shapes and figures to make generalizations regarding congruency, symmetry, and similarity.

If it's been awhile since you explored geometric shapes and figures, here is a glossary of terms to brush up on.

Polygon: a figure with three or more straight sides.

Regular polygon: a polygon with sides of equal length. Some regular polygons can be repeated to make tessellating patterns—that is, the shapes fit together as on a checkerboard or a soccer ball without any space between them.

Quadrilateral: a figure with four sides and four corners. Rectangles and squares are quadrilaterals. (*Note:* The definition of a rectangle is a parallelogram with a right angle; therefore squares are also rectangles.)

Parallel lines: Lines that never intersect no matter how far they extend into space.

Pentagon: a polygon with five sides.

Hexagon: a polygon with six sides.

Octagon: a polygon with eight sides.

pentagon   hexagon   octagon

Congruent: two or more figures that are the exact same size and shape.

Symmetry: A figure that is equally balanced when a line is drawn through a center point.

symmetry

Give your child plenty of practice in exploring these three-dimensional figures:

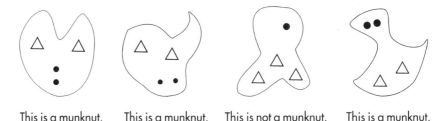

cone   cylinder   cube   sphere   prism

HAVE FIVE MINUTES?

➤ Is your child waiting impatiently for a friend to arrive? Quickly draw four globular shapes on a sheet of paper. Give three of them similar characteristics, make the fourth one different. Tell her that the three that are similar are "munknuts," the one that is different is not. Can she draw a munknut?

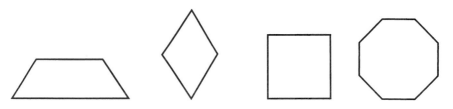

This is a munknut.   This is a munknut.   This is not a munknut.   This is a munknut.

Continue creating new creatures that are distinguishable by number of corners, number of sides or edges, and straight lines or curves. Eventually you can draw shapes that help your child distinguish between shapes that are symmetrical and those that are not, or shapes that have parallel lines and those that do not. Here is another example:

This is a quadrilateral.   This is a quadrilateral.   This is a quadrilateral.   This is not.

➤ Help your child to realize that particular shapes can be categorized in many ways. Think of a specific shape. Now provide clues that help your child slowly narrow down the figure you are thinking of. Here are a couple of examples:

> This figure is a polygon.
> It's a quadrilateral.
> It is symmetrical.
> It has two sets of parallel lines.
> It is not a regular polygon.

or

> This is a solid.
> It has no corners.
> It can be stacked or rolled.
> When one end is traced, it makes a circle.

➤ Photocopy the pattern block cutouts on page 223. Suggest that your third grader trace these on cardboard and then use them as templates to trace again while creating patterns. (Or help her trace and cut two or three of the polygons from a plastic coffee can or margarine lid. The lid then becomes the template.) She can design border patterns—for example, "snowflake patterns" that grow from the center or a tessellating pattern. Encourage her to rotate the shape to view it in different positions. To inspire her exploration, you might suggest that she do one of the following projects:

- Use fabric markers to draw patterns on a pillowcase
- Make stationery with polygon patterns
- Make a place mat; then cover her place mat with clear Con-Tact paper for durability
- Make a poster with a tessellating pattern (introduce your child to the work of M. C. Escher)
- Design wallpaper for a dollhouse or tiles for an action-figure hideout

➤ Suggest that your child discover how many different shapes she can make by gluing five squares together on a sheet of paper (full sides must be touching). After she has made her shapes, have her cut them out and try to fit one on top of another. Are any of her shapes the same when flipped or rotated?

➤ Which of the letters in the alphabet can be rotated 90 or 180 degrees and still look the same? Invite your third grader to find out.

➤ Which of the letters in the alphabet are symmetrical?

➤ Have your third grader try this tavern puzzle: Arrange twelve toothpicks into four congruent squares; then ask your child to rearrange four of the toothpicks to make three congruent squares. (The solution is on page 172.)

➤ Encourage your child to draw a map of her room, her classroom, her house or neighborhood. Discuss how maps are an aerial or bird's-eye view. Ask her to consider what three-dimensional shapes would look like from the sky. If you wish, teach your child about map proportions and have her develop a scale.

HAVE MORE TIME?

➤ Draw the following pattern on paper. Have your child cut the pattern out and, by folding and taping, create a cube. Now ask, "How many different ways can you draw six squares, so that when folded, they create a cube?"

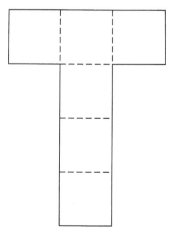

➤If you and your child have already discovered the Attribute Game (page 139) and have gotten quite good at it, you can adapt the game to work with geometry classifications. (If you haven't tried the Attribute game yet, do so now. Children use geometric shapes, size, and color attributes to develop logical reasoning.) To reinforce some of the more sophisticated concepts presented in this section, use the Pattern Block Template and cards found on page 223.

➤If your third grader enjoyed the activity above, have him experiment with folding paper to make a cylinder, a prism, or a cone.

➤Ask your third grader to predict how many sugar squares it would take to build a cube with a length of 2 squares. Then build a cube together to find the answer. Next, have him predict how many cubes it would take to build a cube with the length of 4 and then 6 squares. Have him record his predictions and then build the cubes to compare his predictions with the actual numbers. (If he wishes to create two-dimensional drawings to help him predict the number of cubes, encourage him to use this strategy.)

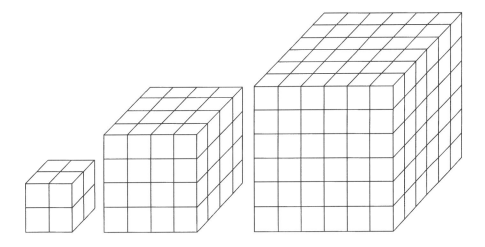

➤When your third grader has had plenty of practice with cubes, challenge him to predict how many cubes it would take to make a $2 \times 4 \times 6$ rectangular solid. Invite him to test his prediction.

➤Design a 9-patch quilt in which each patch is a 9-inch square. Squares, rectangles, and/or parallelograms can be used for the design of each square.

Solution to puzzle on page 170

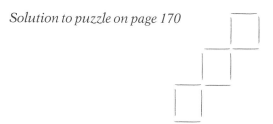

Probability and Statistics

The ability to work with probability and statistics is measured by question 21 on the Math Assessment.

The choice of cereals on the shelf in the grocers, the choice of television shows in your viewing area, the choice of books or fashions available at your local mall, even the medications prescribed to your family are dependent on statistics and probability. Statistics is the collection and organization of relevant information: How many boxes of sugar cereal were sold this year? How many boxes of nuts and grain cereal were sold this year? Probability allows us to predict future trends: Is a new cereal with candy corn likely to sell? In this growing age of information, it's imperative that children, even third graders, begin to understand how information is collected, how data is interpreted, how variables affect validity, and how people draw conclusions based on the information. Here are ways that you can help your child grasp concepts in probability and statistics:

Probability

Probability uses observations and collected data to determine the likelihood of what will happen next. Through experimentation, children learn about patterns and ratios and begin to make predictions based on their firsthand observations.

HAVE MORE TIME?

➤To introduce the concept of probability, let your child watch you place an object, such as a blue Lego block, in a paper bag. Ask, "If I reach in this bag and pull out an object, what are the chances that I will get a blue Lego?" If needed, help him rephrase his answer to tell you that your chances are 100 percent or a 1 in 1 chance. Then place a yellow Lego in the bag and ask, "What are my chances now of reaching in and pulling out a blue Lego?" His response might be 50 percent, half a chance, or 1 in 2. Add a red Lego and then later another blue Lego. If your third grader becomes boggled by the possibilities, have him experiment by reaching in the bag forty times and recording which block he pulls out each time. What conclusions does he reach? It is not important that your child learn the specific odds, but that he simply gets experience in thinking about possibilities.

➤ Going on a long car ride? Bring along that paper bag and Lego blocks. Have your third grader pull out a block and record its color ten times. (Make sure he returns the block to the bag before drawing another.) Then have him predict what colors are in the bag and in what proportion: "I think there are yellow, red, and black Legos in the bag. There are more red than yellow or black." He'll love checking his predictions.

➤ Suggest that your third grader toss a coin several times and record the number of times the coin lands on heads or tails. Encourage him to record the results in his own way. After he has had a few minutes to experiment, ask him to predict whether heads or tails will come up more with ten tosses. Twenty-five tosses? Fifty tosses? Have him check his predictions.

> Look for the book *Do You Wanna Bet?: Your Chance to Find Out About Probability*, by Jean Cushman (Clarion), at your local library, for an entertaining way to look at this subject.

Here are some questions you might ask:
- What are your chances of coming up with tails? Heads?
- How did you record the results of your coin toss? Did it work well?
- Would you use the same recording method if you were to try this experiment again?
- Would you get the same results if you did this activity over again?
- If the chances of getting heads or tails are equal, does that mean that you will always get heads half the time and tails half the time?

➤ Next time you're in the grocery line, startle your child by picking up a package of colored candies. Place six red and three yellow in your hand. Invite your child to predict what color candy he will get when he reaches in your curled hand to pick one. Who says math isn't fun?

➤ Play a quick game in which each of you tries to set the record for the most rolls on two dice without rolling doubles. This game could go on all day!

➤ Suggest that your child choose a paragraph from any book and predict which letters are used most. Then have her tally how many times each letter appears. Encourage her to design a graph to show her results.

➤ Don't forget to explore combinations with your child. While exploring a definite number of possibilities, children recognize patterns and gain a more intuitive knowledge of numbers. When your third grader is begging for a new number puzzle or experiment, suggest one of these:

- If there are six pizza toppings available, and you have enough money to buy a pizza with two toppings, how many different choices of pizza do you have?
- The ice cream parlor has four different kinds of ice cream and three sauces. How many different sundaes could you have?
- If there are five ballerinas, and the director would like three to appear in one scene, how many combinations of dancers can she choose from?
- You have been asked to create a painting using only four colors. There are eight different tubes of paint to choose from, how many possible color combinations do you have?

➤ Play the Odd and Even game. One of you is Odd, the other Even. Say, "One, two, three, shoot," and simultaneously show 1, 2, or 3 fingers on one hand. If the sum is odd, Odd gets a point. If the sum is even, Even gets a point. After you have played for a few rounds, have your child make a chart that shows the chances of the sum being odd or even. Who will your child choose to be next time? Does it make a difference?

HAVE MORE TIME?

➤ Play Pig. One of the nice things about exploring statistics and probability is that it provides practice in many other skills. This traditional game will not only get your child thinking about chance, but you will sharpen his abilities to use mental arithmetic.

PIG

1. Player A begins a round by rolling the dice as many times as he wishes, and adding the two numbers together. Player A may stop his round at any point and record the sum on paper. Then it's Player B's turn.
2. On Player A's next round, he begins adding on to the sum recorded last.
3. If, on any turn, a player rolls a one, he gets a zero for that round. (But he keeps his prior sum.)
4. If, on any turn, a player rolls snake eyes (double ones), his round ends and his overall total returns to zero.
5. The first player to reach 100 is the winner.

➤ Here is a game of probability that will help your third grader use strategic thinking. You will need a horizontal grid with the numbers 1 to 12 and 12 beans or pennies for counters. Have your child place the counters anywhere on the grid. He can place one counter on each number, or several counters on one number, and no counters on another. Then have him roll the dice and remove the sum from the grid. If there is no counter on that sum, he rolls again. Have him record the number of rolls it takes to remove all 12 counters. Can he beat his score? Encourage him to keep trying. If he wishes, take turns trying to remove the counters in fewer rolls. Share your strategies for placing the counters.

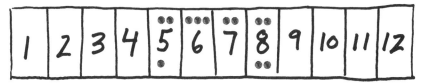

Statistics

Kindergarten and first and second graders learn to gather information by asking questions about things that relate to them: How many pets do you have? What is your favorite vegetable? They also learn ways to record information (tallies, real graphs, picture graphs, bar graphs) and how to interpret the data: How many children have dogs? Cats? How many more children have goldfish than cats?

Third graders are ready and able to use this growing knowledge of statistics to alter their thinking and their world. In addition to personal surveys, they are interested in seeking information relevant to their social environment: How many students are buying hot lunch? How much paper does our school recycle? How long does it take for third graders to complete homework at night? They learn more options for recording information (pie graphs, line graphs, frequency charts) and they make decisions regarding which recording form is best to use in particular situations. Once they've interpreted the information, they take the analysis of it one step farther: How come more students aren't buying hot lunch on Fridays? How could we get more classrooms to recycle? How much time should third graders spend on homework? Is our class above or below the recommended time? Statistics allow them to draw conclusions about what they know and to discover what they need to learn next.

Help your child to see that different kinds of graphs serve different purposes. For instance, bar graphs and circle graphs help us to compare information. Line graphs show changes over time. If you have access to computer software with graphing capabilities, you may want to show your third grader how to use it. As we all know, creating graphs by hand can sometimes be time consuming. The computer allows us to plug in data and get quick visual results.

HAVE FIVE MINUTES?

➤ **Record Data** "But Mom, I don't need a sweater. I was boiling at lunch recess!" Instead of repeating the temperature change lecture for the umpteenth time, why not suggest that your child keep a record of daily temperatures for two weeks? Having children collect data over time can help them develop the critical thinking skills necessary to interpret data. Invite your child to choose some of the ideas listed below that interest her. Have her predict what the graph will look like before she begins. Once she starts recording data, ask her to point out any changes and to speculate the reasons for the changes. For instance, if your child is plotting her bedtime over a course of a month, ask her to tell you why she thinks Friday nights are always later than the other nights.

- Record the temperature at three different times of the day for two weeks and plot the results on a line graph. Do you see any patterns? What conclusions can you draw?
- Make a rain or snow gauge. Check the gauge daily and plot the results on a line graph. Next time you're at the library, compare this year's precipitation with last year's. What conclusions can you draw? Are two years' statistics enough to determine the weather patterns in your area?
- Record your bedtime for a month. Do you see any patterns?

➤ The next time you're entertaining a large group, have your child take a survey. She can begin by tallying the number of people who wear black, or like olives, or have heard of her favorite book. Encourage her to come up with her own survey questions. What would she really like to know?

HAVE MORE TIME?

➤ Your third grader will probably do a lot more reading of circle graphs this year than creating them, unless he has access to graphing software. Nevertheless, you can give him the chance to think about proportions in a circle graph. Here's one way. Pull out your junk drawer and suggest that he divide the objects in the drawer into three groups. He can make up the rules for sorting, such as tools to write with, tools to fasten with, and tools to power things. (You may need to suggest that one category be "other" depending on the range of items in your drawer.) After he has sorted the junk according to his rules, have him make a circle graph showing the size relationships between the groups. At this stage, it is not important for him to demonstrate the exact fraction each group represents, only the size comparisons.

Introduction to Division

Your child's understanding of basic division is assessed by questions 19 and 20 on the Math Assessment.

Should third graders learn division? There are two camps when the question is raised. The first camp feels that multiplication and division are related activities, and that it would be foolish to spend time teaching one without the other. The second camp feels that the concept of division remains a difficult one for most eight-year-olds, and that if we simply wait one more year, children will grasp the concept with more understanding and less effort. Both camps, however, agree that memorizing division facts should not be expected in third grade (though some children will immediately grasp division facts as they memorize the multiplication table).

> ### BOOKS THAT INTRODUCE DIVISION
>
> Many families are familiar with the Pat Hutchins book *The Doorbell Rang* (Greenwillow). This is a great book for teaching the concept of division. Other books you might want to look for are *One Hundred Hungry Ants* and *A Remainder of One*, both by Elinor J. Pinzes (Houghton Mifflin). These books help children understand the process of division in a lively, entertaining way.

If your child is having an easy time of multiplication and you would like to introduce her to division, do so, not by showing her the symbols of division (÷, ⌐) and providing workbooks, but by presenting concrete experiences and real division problems. Keep in mind as you do this that there are two different types of division problems: (1) beginning with a known quantity and dividing it into equal parts ("If there are thirty goldfish crackers and five children, how many crackers can each child have?") and (2) knowing the size of the groups and determining how many groups make up a collection ("If baseball cards come four per pack, and you want to collect thirty-six cards, how many packs of baseball cards do you need to buy?") Your child does not need to distinguish between these two, but you should keep them in mind as you present a variety of problems to your child.

When children are just starting to solve division problems, they often use the operations they are most comfortable with. For instance, to find out how many baseball packs are needed to collect thirty-six cards, your child might use this approach:

4 + 4 + 4 + 4 + 4 + 4 + 4 + 4 + 4 = 36
Or
$4 \times 2 = 8$ $8 + 8 + 8 + 8 + 8 = 40$ $40 - 4 = 36$
Or
$4 \times 9 = 36$

Don't worry about how much time your child takes, or the operations she chooses to use. All of these approaches will help teach her about division.

Remember, division is crucial to the understanding of fractions, percentages, and decimals. You do not want to shortchange her learning by teaching her simple facts too soon. Instead, explore division in these fun and challenging ways.

HAVE FIVE MINUTES?

➤ Next time you're setting out a plate of cookies, have your child determine how many cookies each person may have. Do the same whenever stickers, pennies, or balloons are being divvied up. Before your child deals out the cards for games such as Add! (page 146), have him determine how many cards each person will get.

➤ Have your child invent division story problems for you to solve. Creating problems helps children see when a certain function, such as division, is needed.

➤ Help your child visualize division problems, especially those with remainders. Have him make *x*'s or dots to represent the quotient. Next, have him draw circles around groups that equal the divisor. Your third grader will be able to see that not all whole numbers can be divided into equal groups.

➤ Create story problems for your child: "While James was walking to school one day, he found sixty cents on the ground. He offered to share the money with his five friends. How much did each friend get? Did you remember to leave some for James? What if he was suddenly joined by another friend? Now how much does each child get?"

➤ Ask your child to predict which numbers between 20 and 30 have more factors (not counting 1 and the number itself). For example, the factors of 21 are 3 and 7. The factors of 24 are 2, 3, 4, 6, 8, and 12. Twenty-four has more factors than 21. Suggest that she keep a chart to make comparisons.

➤ If your third grader enjoyed the last challenge, suggest she find common multiples. For instance, she could find 3 common multiples for 3 and 6 (12, 18, 24).

Working Below Grade Level in Math

If you are worried about your child's progress in math, it's probably a new concern. Most problems regarding mathematical ability do not become apparent until the third grade, and often much later. Teachers understand that the acquisition of mathematical understanding requires maturation. Children must reach a certain developmental stage, for instance, to understand conservation of volume and number. They also need a good deal of interaction with concrete materials before they can grasp symbolic concepts. Usually, children in first and second grade are provided with lots of opportunities to explore. Math programs at these levels do well to support the child who requires the manipulation of concrete objects while working with math concepts. And in most cases, the curricula does not demand that children memorize a multitude of procedures that are not supported by experience first.

At the third grade level, however, there is a transition. Often children spend less time working with manipulatives. They are expected to perform more procedures (addition with regrouping, subtraction with renaming, multiplication, division with remainders) and they are presented with an ever-increasing vocabulary to memorize (parallel lines, congruent, probability). In short, the curricula now demands that children extend their thinking (and hopefully understanding) in new and increasingly difficult ways.

If your child is suddenly reporting that he doesn't like math, that math is boring, or that he doesn't "get it," now is the time to take action. Do not accept these remarks as typical student complaints. Yes, math can be hard. But it is usually perceived as difficult (as opposed to challenging) by the child who has stopped making connections, who has stopped experiencing success. When a child has lost ground in mathematical comprehension, it is hard to catch up.

So why has your child lost ground? Here are some possible reasons.

Maturation

Some children (and often very bright children) are simply developmentally younger than their peers. These children require additional time to acquire the "hooks" and critical thinking skills necessary to make sense of math. If your child is young, you and/or your child's teacher are probably seeing evidence of this in other areas of his life. Schedule a time to talk to this teacher about your concerns. In the meantime, provide time at home to work with concrete materials. By choosing many of the hands-on experiences described in this book, you can help your child link the concepts he's learning at home with the math problems he's facing in school.

Lack of Concrete Experience

If your child's math experience heretofore has consisted of math worksheets and workbooks, without a good deal of practice in working with manipulatives, it's likely that he has worked hard at memorizing procedures (borrow a one from the tens column) but does not genuinely know why or how these procedures work. No one can get far in math by memorizing procedures or tricks alone. There are just too many tricks to learn. And problem solving, which is a growing part of American math education, requires children to understand the reasons behind the processes. An inability to explain a process, an inability to solve a problem in more than one way, an inability to apply what has been learned to new problems signals a need for more work with concrete materials. Again, search for those activities in this book (usually the first ones in each list) that suggest ways to connect mathematical learning to real problems in the real world. Give your child concrete objects to help him make the necessary connections. Pattern blocks, base-ten blocks, and tiles—with directions on how to help your child learn mathematical concepts—are available at many toy stores or through catalogs. Ironically, parents who want to boost their child's skills in math often buy workbooks. For the child who is struggling to complete work pages at school, that is the quickest way to kill his interest in or success with math.

Math Anxiety

Does your child express distress at the mere sight of a new math problem? Does she label herself a "bad at math" kid? If this is the case, she may be experiencing what educators and psychologists recognize as math anxiety. Math anxiety can affect any student, but it is far more likely to interfere with a girl's process than with a boy's. There is a good deal of speculation as to why this is so. One reason may be that we simply expect boys to be better at math. We lower our expectations of girls, give them less time to solve problems on their own, and even go so far as to do problems for them! In addition, boys are more often provided with toys that develop spatial awareness such as blocks, Lincoln logs, Legos, and Kinex. As a parent of a child with math anxiety, your first job is to examine your own biases (gender or otherwise) about math. Do you frequently tell your child, "Don't bring your homework to me. I was never good at math"? Do you let her off the hook: "Don't worry. Most girls struggle with math," or infer that she'll never need to use it anyway? As you've probably seen in other areas, parental values can have a tremendous effect (good or bad) on how a child views herself as a doer and a learner. Instead of transferring your anxiety to your child, rediscover math right along with her. This time, discover the fun and the joy that comes with grasping new concepts and finding creative solutions to problems. Play some of the games listed on pages 141–44. When she comes home from school, ask, "Do you have any math for us to do together tonight?" And convey the understanding that the two of you can get it if you just put your minds to it.

A Learning Disability

Children can have learning difficulties that affect their memory and their organizational skills—two areas that are necessary for successful learning of mathematics. ADD (Attention Deficit Disorder) and hyperactivity can impede a child's ability to concentrate on math work. So can a reading disorder, such as dyslexia, since children need to read directions and word problems effectively in order to understand them. Learning disabilities are often masked by what appear to be normal problems such as sloppy work, daydreaming, or acting out. When trying to pinpoint the source of your child's frustration, remember that most children would rather succeed than not succeed. They would rather feel good about themselves than hear constant reminders and/or criticisms. If you suspect that a disability is getting in the way of your child's success, do not hesitate to get in touch with your child's teacher. Make that appointment now.

"I Hate to Write!"

What does hating to write have to do with math achievement? Lately, plenty. For good reasons, many math programs focus on *how* children learn mathematical concepts and *how* they find solutions instead of simply filling in correct answers on worksheets. Subsequently, children are asked to write about the strategies they use and what they discover. Those children who have previously excelled in math, for whom problem solving comes easy, yet who consider writing the severest form of torture, now find math their nemesis. These children tend to be stronger in logical-mathematical intelligence than linguistic intelligence. How does a child who can "see" an answer in her head in a matter of seconds explain how she got it? How can a child who has the persistence to stay with a problem and try a number of tactics record it effectively? If your child reads puzzle books at home, makes up her own math problems to solve, and can figure out the grocery bill before you but is not succeeding in school, you may want to talk to her teacher about an alternative method of recording learning. Permission to use a tape recorder or to draw charts may help your child get back on track.

Although the reasons a child may be having difficulty in math are varied, there are some strategies that might help her until you've identified the bigger picture. Skim the ideas below and see if any would work for your child and her particular situation:

HAVE FIVE MINUTES?

➤ If you know that your child needs more time with concrete instruction than you can provide, consider hiring a tutor. The tutor could be a former teacher, a person who specializes in helping children succeed in school, or simply a high school student who would be willing to play the appropriate games with your child. Many a baby-sitter would be happy to play 500 (page 149) or Pig (page 174) with your child.

➤ When your child brings home a math worksheet, suggest that instead of beginning at the top of the page and working to the bottom, she choose the problems she would like to do first. By completing some of the problems successfully, her confidence is raised and she's ready to tackle the rest.

➤ If she has difficulty lining her problems up (many errors occur when the numbers do not appear in the correct columns), have her use lined paper turned horizontally. The lines will provide columns.

➤ When it comes to regrouping or "carrying" in addition, some children have difficulty separating the tens from the ones. (They forget that the number on the left represents tens.) Instead of carrying the number to the top of the problem, have your child try carrying it *below* the problem as shown.

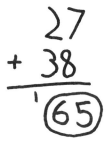

➤ If your child has a math paper that involves a different function (addition, subtraction, multiplication), color code the problems for her. For instance, you might use a red highlighter to go over the addition signs, a green highlighter to go over the subtraction signs, and a yellow highlighter to signal "multiplication is coming."

➤ Read *Math Curse,* by Jon Scieszka (Viking). This story will quickly convince you that all of life is a math problem and you'll get plenty of practice in critical math thinking as you explore it together.

➤ Another story that you might want to check out is *The Flunking of Joshua T. Bates,* by Susan Shreve (Bullseye Books). Joshua, the smartest kid in the third grade, is developmentally young and forced to repeat the year— lucky thing for Joshua.

HAVE MORE TIME?

➤ Play with puzzles of any kind. Puzzles help a child develop spatial awareness and reward persistence. Make sure, however, that you show the child what the puzzle looks like whole, and allow her to work from a visual model (the picture on the box) while putting it together.

Math Enrichment

Children who excel in math seem to have "instant knowledge." When asked how they got their answer, many respond, "I just knew it." They see patterns and logical connections that go unnoticed by others. And they have an uncanny drive to learn more. They don't mind being challenged and can occupy themselves for days with a persnickety problem. Once they're on a mathematical trail, they won't let up. You may marvel at your child's concentration when engaged with a math puzzle and wonder what happened to that ability to concentrate when he has a chore to do.

But sharing these traits with other children who achieve in math doesn't necessarily mean that they were born with them. Believing that mathematical ability is innate—you're either born with it or you're not—is a limiting and sometimes damaging belief. Children who are taught to play a sport or a musical instrument often develop an intrinsic motivation and the desire to learn more. They form a passion that lasts a lifetime. With the right kind of nurturing, children can discover the joy of math. If your child tells you, "Margaret goes to gifted and talented math," ask, "Would you like to work toward getting into that program?" There's no guarantee your child will eventually qualify, but there's no guarantee that she'll end up on the basketball team either. Both take commitment, effort, and, perhaps most of all, a mentor. You can be that mentor.

If your child's ready for a challenge, focus on helping him learn with depth, not just breadth. Instead of purchasing fourth or even fifth grade workbooks (that are likely to provide boring drill activities), consider applying the concepts your child has learned this year to new and exciting problems. (The difference between math instruction in the United States and other countries is that while American schools cover more topics in math, they are studied in far less time and in less depth. This may be one reason why American children on the whole trail in numeracy.)

Mathematical learning, like most learning, is fostered when children have the opportunity to work with like minds. So jump into the action, or help your child find a friend who also loves being a mathematical sleuth. Look for weekend classes that provide mathematical fun and explore math exhibits at local museums and libraries. Here are a few more ideas to keep you going at home.

HAVE FIVE MINUTES?

➤ Explore negative numbers. Your child may have some understanding of negative numbers on a number line, but ask, "When do we use negative numbers?" With some time to ponder this question, he may come up with temperature, floors in a building below the ground floor, and credit or money owed. Suggest that he make up a game that involves negative numbers. (Please note that this concept may remain too abstract for many third graders. If your child doesn't grasp the concept, try again in a few months.)

➤ Give your child challenging math problems and suggest she check her answers on a calculator. But there's one rule: She can only use the inverse operation. For instance, if you gave her a multiplication problem, she would have to use division to check her answer.

➤ Introduce your third grader to Pascal's triangle. Ask, "How would you extend this pattern?"

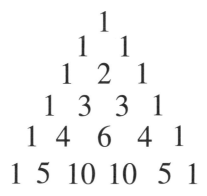

➤ If your child is ready for a challenge in multiplication, introduce him to factorials, which are the product of all the positive numbers between one and a given number. For example, 3 factorial, written 3!, is $1 \times 2 \times 3 = 6$. Challenge your child to see how high he can go with factorials.

➤ Proportion is another area that you can study, given your third grader's knowledge of numbers. See if she can find the answers to these problems:

5 is to 10 as 4 is to _____ (8)

12 is to 4 as 9 is to _____ (3)

16 is to 4 as 4 is to _____ (1)

➤ This favorite puzzle will keep your third grader busy for hours (but will only take you a minute to introduce). Using the number sequence one through nine, and the addition and subtraction symbols, ask how many number sentences can you think of that equal 100? Here's one: $1 + 2 + 3 - 4 + 5 + 6 + 78 + 9 = 100$.

➤ Show your child how to determine the area of a triangle. Have him draw a triangle on graph paper. Then demonstrate how to draw a rectangle around the triangle. Ask him to compare the number of spaces within the triangle to those in the entire rectangle. What has he learned about determining the area of a triangle? (The area of the triangle is half the area of the rectangle.) Have him experiment to see if his conclusions always work.

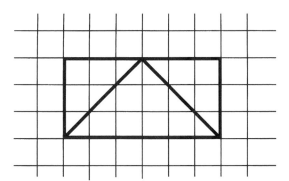

➤ Photocopy the pattern block templates on page 223. Then have your child choose a shape, trace it ten times on paper, and cut all of the traced shapes out. Have her record the perimeter of one shape. Then suggest that she put two of these shapes together so that two faces are touching. What is the perimeter now? Try three shapes. Now what's the perimeter? Have her predict the pattern for adding shapes four through ten. Then have her check her prediction.

➤ Do you have a letter scale? Have your curious third grader find combinations of items that equal precisely one pound. How many combinations can he find?

HAVE MORE TIME?

➤ Using toothpicks and frozen peas, invite your child to make three-dimensional polygons. She might want to play with making two-dimensional sides first and then connect them to make a three-dimensional figure. Don't ask your child to stick to geometric shapes she's studying, instead let her create the design of her heart.

➤ Using two different colored dice, how many combinations could your child roll for the numbers 2 through 12? For instance, with the number 5, he could roll 1 + 4, 4 + 1, 2 + 3, 3 + 2—that's 4 combinations. Have him make a chart of his results. What patterns does he see? What conclusions can he draw? After he has determined that there are 36 different combinations in all, point out that he has a 4 in 36, or a 4/36, chance of rolling a 5. What are his chances of rolling a 10?

➤ If you have access to a computer program with spreadsheet capability, teach your budding statistician to use it. She might record the daily temperatures, the minutes the dog was walked, the amount of money received for returned bottles. Once she gets going, she'll probably have lots of ideas of her own.

➤ Encourage your child to create her own board game. You might want to brainstorm a list of what makes a good game, then extend your thinking. Will you use dice? If so, what if you could choose to add or subtract the number rolled on the dice? What if you could multiply your roll? What if you had a limited number of rolls (days on a journey)? File folders make wonderful game boards and are handy for the child who has many ideas.

➤ Play a game of fraction war. Deal out all cards from aces to tens (remove jacks, queens, and kings) to two or more players. All players turn over their top two cards and make a proper fraction (less than one, smaller number on top). The player who makes the greater fraction takes all the cards and keeps them on the bottom of her pile. The player who gets all the cards wins.

Working with Your Child's Teacher

This book and the accompanying assessment can provide you with lots of information about third grade expectations and how your own child is progressing toward meeting them. There is, however, much information about your child's schooling that this book cannot provide.

This book cannot tell you, for example, the methods your child's teacher uses to teach third grade skills. Does she teach to the large group, to small groups, or individuals? Does she encourage children to work together, or does she ask them to work alone, or both? This book also cannot tell you the sequence in which the skills will be taught or integrated into the curriculum. Will measurement be introduced in the beginning of the year or at the end? What math skills will be incorporated into the unit on Japan?

No book can tell you exactly how your child's performance is being measured and recorded this year since assessment methods vary greatly from school to school, and from classroom to classroom. No book can give you a clear picture of how your child interacts in the classroom (you may discover that your child behaves quite differently in different settings) or how your child is doing socially. Both of these factors greatly affect school success.

To gather this kind of information, you must have a strong line of communication with your child's teacher. Most schools provide several ways for teachers and parents to share information, but you may discover that you can glean far more information if you take the lead now and then. Here are some ways to get a closer look at your child's learning experience.

Open House

Open house, also known as parents' night or back-to-school night, is an evening set aside for teachers to present their goals, methods of instruction, and routines. The purpose of this event is not to discuss individual students but to introduce the program and classroom procedures as a whole.

Open house presentations are as varied as the personalities of the teachers who give them. Your child's teacher may present you with a brief written description of his expectations, or he may simply invite you to come into the room and look around. He may have you participate in some of the math and reading activities the children do, or he may have a video or a slide show to demonstrate a typical day in his third grade classroom.

If your child's teacher has not prepared an elaborate or particularly detailed presentation, do remember that not all teachers are extroverts. Many feel far more comfortable in a room with twenty-five rambunctious eight-year-olds than in front of a group of adults. If this is true of your child's teacher, try posing a few encouraging questions to help him provide you and other appreciative parents with more detailed information.

"But," you might say, "what if I am not an extrovert either? And besides, I don't want the teacher to think I'm an overbearing or uncooperative parent!" Indeed, many parents find that they are more anxious on parents' night than the teachers are. The parents' own experiences as students or their lingering fear of authority may cause trepidation. After all, whose heart doesn't beat a little faster at the thought of being sent to the principal's office? Simply meeting the person with whom your child will spend over 180 days this year can be unnerving enough to cause you to sit passively at your child's desk.

Keep in mind that *how* you pose your questions can make a difference. Questions need not be challenges. They can be invitations. "What do land forms have to do with addition and subtraction?" is a challenge. On the other hand, "Your study of land forms sounds fascinating. Can you tell us more about the ways you will integrate math skills into that study?" is an invitation to discussion. Most teachers are passionate about children and the subjects they teach. Encourage your child's teacher to expound on what excites him most.

Parent Conferences

There are three kinds of parent-teacher conferences: regularly scheduled conferences, special conferences that you initiate, and special conferences that your teacher initiates. The purpose of each is the same: to discuss how your child is doing and how you can support him emotionally and educationally.

Your role in each of these, however, will vary depending upon who initiated the conference.

Scheduled Conferences

Scheduled conferences usually occur once at the beginning of the school year and once later on in the year. Before attending a scheduled conference, you'll want to do some data gathering. Remember, the more information you have going into a conference, the easier the conference will be for everyone. Begin with your child. Long before conference time, you should be asking specific questions. "How's school going?" may not elicit much of a response. But specific questions, such as these, might prompt a more meaningful response:

- What books are you reading in school?
- What's your favorite thing to do in class? Why?
- What do you like best (or least) about math?
- Does your teacher call on you very often?
- What worries you about school?

Next, think about learning activities you and your child have done together, and any questions the activities have raised. If you have given your child the assessment in this book, you may find that you already have a number of questions. For instance, you may have observed that your child approaches math problems by recalling a procedure: "First I do this. Then I do this." Even if the teacher reports that your child is doing well in math, you might want to discuss whether your child is memorizing ways to solve problems or whether he truly understands the way numbers work. Tell the teacher what you have observed at home, and see if your observations match the teacher's.

As you prepare the questions you wish to ask your child's teacher, be aware that the teacher herself is preparing to meet with more than twenty sets of parents. It is likely that she has established a routine, such as showing you samples of your child's work or the results of formal and informal assessments. She may have one or two issues she wishes to bring to your attention. Because of the uniformity of these conferences, you might find yourself wondering if the teacher truly knows your child. A comment such as "Your son is such a pleasure to have in class" is nice to hear. But it is not nearly as useful—and ultimately as cherished—as "Your son has read all the beginning mysteries in the classroom and is now gobbling up books about space." To elicit more specific comments about your child, feel free to ask questions like:

- In what areas have you seen the most growth? The least?
- How does my child's performance compare with that of other children at this grade level? (Teachers understandably do not like to compare children and are often reluctant to answer this question, but it is an important one. Keep in mind that you need to know about your child's progress

and performance. The teacher may tell you that your child is growing daily as a reader. But until you know that the growth that is taking place is in the lowest reading group, you have only half the picture.)

- What are my child's work habits like?
- What are my child's interests?
- What motivates my child in school?
- Does my child have special friends? What are they like?
- How would you describe my child's attention span?
- What can I be doing at home to help support my child's learning?

If, during the conference, the teacher uses jargon with which you're not familiar, or if the teacher describes your child in ways that seem vague, ask for clarification. "A live wire" could mean that your child is bright and curious or that he has difficulty sitting still or paying attention. Try not to leave the conference until you are sure you have a clear picture.

Most routine conferences are scheduled in fifteen- to twenty-minute blocks (which is why you want to be on time for yours). If your conference is coming to an end and you have just unearthed an area of concern, ask to schedule another conference. Most teachers will be happy to do so.

You may find that your child is invited or expected to attend the teacher's conference with you. This format has both its advantages and disadvantages. By attending the conference, your child will be encouraged to take a more active role in his own learning and assessment. But you may have questions you would like to discuss with the teacher privately. If your child has been asked to attend, and you do not want to discuss all of your concerns in his presence, request a second appointment or indicate that you will be following up with a phone call.

When You Initiate a Conference

Although you may be tempted to seek information from the teacher during a class field trip or while you're dropping your child off at school after a dentist appointment, try to refrain from doing so. Impromptu discussions about one child's progress are too much to ask of a teacher who's fully immersed in teaching. Instead, if you have concerns or wish to know more about your child's learning, make an appointment to see the teacher or speak with her on the telephone.

You may want to schedule a conference or phone call to inform the teacher of any stresses or special circumstances your child is experiencing. Illness, parental separation or divorce, death of a dear one (including pets), and particular fears can all affect a child's school experience and are well worth revealing to the teacher. It is also appropriate to schedule a conference if you have noticed confusing or unwarranted changes in your child's behavior. Together you and the teacher may be able to pull together enough information to make sense of the change.

At times, your concerns may have less to do with your child's individual progress than with the classroom situation as a whole. Perhaps you take issue with a specific method your child's teacher is using, or you would like to see learning addressed in other ways. Parents often hesitate to talk to teachers about these considerations for fear that the teacher will feel attacked and subsequently take her anger out on their child. This common fear is rarely warranted. Teachers know that listening and responding to parents will ultimately bring about more support, not less. In most situations, a concern, particularly a first-time concern, is taken quite seriously, especially if your choice of words and tone of voice are cooperative rather than confrontational. In schools, as in other institutions, the squeaky wheel does get the grease. Scheduling a conference and expressing your concern in a genuine spirit of collaboration is appropriate.

If you have a concern about your child and are wondering if you should set up a conference, do so, and do it *now*. (October is not too soon.) It is far better to communicate early, when both you and your child's teacher can be proactive, rather than reactive. Address the problem *before* your child experiences frustration or a sense of failure. Success is the leading motivator in school achievement. Don't let your child lose that feeling of success.

When the Teacher Initiates a Conference

Suppose you come home from work to find a message on your answering machine from your child's teacher asking for a conference. Like any parent, you assume the worst. First comes the flood of questions for your child: How are things going at school? Any problems? Next comes the flow of parental guilt: What have I failed to do?

Don't panic. Find out the specific purpose of the meeting. Who knows? Your child's teacher may simply want to talk to you about a volunteer position in the classroom or about your child's special talents. If she seems reluctant to give you details before a meeting, understand that this is to prevent an immediate and full-range discussion at the time of the phone call. In truth, it is probably more advantageous for everyone involved to wait, process the information, and be prepared at the meeting. To find out the purpose of the meeting, you might say, "I know that we don't have time to discuss the issue now, but could you tell me in a few words what the conference will be about?" Then ask who, other than the teacher, will attend the conference. Finally, ask, "Is there a helpful way that I can prepare?" This last question will set the right tone, indicating that you are open and eager to work together.

If two parents are involved in your child's education, try to arrange for both of you to attend the conference. This way one parent will not end up trying to communicate information secondhand, and everyone can become involved in a plan of action. Be sure to arrange a means for following up as well. You may want to set up a regular system of communication—sending notes back and forth, perhaps, or calling every Friday. Some teachers even suggest keeping a "dialogue journal" in which the parent and teacher exchange progress reports and observations in a notebook that the child carries to and from school.

Whether you initiate a conference or the teacher does, remember that the main purpose of any conference is to collect and share essential information. More often than not, teachers are relieved when parents bring problems to their attention. You, too, should be glad that a problem has been noticed and addressed. At the very least, by opening a vital line of communication, you and the teacher will clarify important views pertaining to the education of your child.

Student Assessment

When you went to school there were probably two types of assessments: tests and report cards. The same holds true for many schools today. In some schools, primary students do not take tests—except perhaps for the weekly spelling test—but they do get report cards. The report card may have letter grades; it may be a checklist; or it might be an anecdotal report. In still other schools, new methods of evaluation, called performance-based testing or authentic assessment, use anecdotal records, learning journals, and portfolios as a means of reporting progress. A third type of assessment is the standardized test. Each type of assessment looks at learning from one or more angles, and all can be helpful to you and your child if you understand the benefits and limitations of each form.

Report Cards

Report cards are often considered a conclusion: How well did your child do this quarter? How hard did she try? Many types of report cards, however, raise more questions than they answer. If your child gets grades, you may find yourself wondering what a B really means. Is your child performing slightly above the average for the whole class? Or is your child performing slightly above average in her math group? Can a child in the lowest math group get a B? If your child doesn't get traditional letter grades, but receives an *O* for outstanding, *S* for satisfactory, and an *N* for needs improvement, you may still be left wondering what constitutes an outstanding grade as opposed to a satisfactory one.

Many schools are moving toward more informative report cards. These usually include a checklist of skills and learning behaviors and are marked according to how often your child exhibits those behaviors (consistently, most of the time, sometimes, not yet). The checklist may also be accompanied by anecdotal records. Remember, the perfect reporting device for all children has yet to be devised. Report cards are designed for parents, so if the reports in your district do not meet your needs, let the principal know.

No matter what type of report card your child receives, try to use it as a springboard rather than as a conclusion. As a springboard, a report card gives you the opportunity to talk with your child. Here are some suggestions:

- Ask your child what she thinks of this progress report. Listen to his feelings and guide him in assessing how he thinks he's doing.
- First and foremost, praise your child for things done well. In fact, you may want to concentrate only on the positive in your first reaction to a report card.
- If you and your child can see a place that needs improvement, talk about *how* he can go about improving. Telling him to try harder or giving him incentives (a dollar for every A) are probably not helpful. He cannot improve without a clear understanding of what is expected of him and how he can work on the problem.
- If you have already pinpointed a need using the assessment in this book, the report card can provide an opportunity to reinforce the good work you have already begun to do together. Tell your child that you are proud of his extra effort.
- If you have questions about the report card or if you need further clarification, schedule a conference with your child's teacher.

Above all, keep your discussion with your child as upbeat and positive as possible. Remember, report cards can tear down what your child needs most: confidence. So as your child's main coach, review the report card, but don't let it define him or give him the impression that your love or respect is based on his ability. Your child is not an A or a C student. He is what we all are, continuous learners.

Performance-Based Assessment

In many schools, teachers are pushing for changes in assessment. They realize that learning does not just occur at the end of a unit or the end of a marking period. It is happening all the time. In these schools, teachers are keeping records while observing children at work. They talk to children about what they know and how they approach problems. In addition, both students and their teachers often save the work that demonstrates learning and keep it in a portfolio.

A portfolio is a collection of work. It may contain several writing samples (usually the rough drafts in addition to the finished product to show growth), charts and descriptions that show how a child approached a math or science project, drawings or other art work, and a report or project done over time. Sometimes the teacher chooses what will go into the portfolio, sometimes the child decides, and sometimes they select the work together. In any case, the student is usually asked to do some self-assessment.

Most parents find portfolios a good source of information about their child's progress and school expectations. They are able to see the quality of their child's thinking, the effort that was applied, and the outcomes. While reviewing a portfolio, parents and teachers can discuss future goals for the child.

If your child's teacher isn't using a portfolio method, but regularly sends home completed work, you can assemble your own portfolio. Some parents buy artists' portfolios for this purpose, others use accordion files or date the work and keep it in a cardboard box. Study the work in the portfolio for signs of how your child is progressing. Go beyond the teacher's comments at the top of the paper, and look instead for changes in the child's work. Praise her for applying new concepts and showing what she knows. As you do the exercises in this book, keep work that demonstrates growth. These may come in handy when you are discussing your child's needs with the teacher.

Standardized Testing

Standardized tests can be administered to children as early as kindergarten. However, their validity is less reliable in the early primary grades. Young children are inexperienced in taking tests. They have difficulty following directions and predicting correct test responses. Some schools give practice tests in kindergarten or in grades one or two. Other schools wait until the second or third grade before having children participate in standardized testing.

Standardized tests are considered "objective"—they are administered in the same manner, with the same directions, to children at the same grade level all across the country. They measure student performance in norms, percentiles, and stanines that allow children to be compared to other children, and schools to be compared with other schools. The results of standardized tests can be used—and are used—in a number of different ways. Some of the most common uses are: to determine the strengths and weaknesses of the educational program; to inform teachers and parents about the academic growth of individual students; and to identify children who may have learning problems or who may need a more challenging school experience. (Standardized test scores are often used as the criteria to select children who need additional support at either end of the learning continuum.)

If your child will participate in standardized testing this year, prepare her by briefly discussing the purpose of the test in a low-key manner—"to help your teacher decide what to teach next and to help your teacher teach you well"— and by making sure that your child has plenty of sleep the night before the test and a good breakfast that morning. It's in your child's best interest not to put too much emotional weight on the test or the test results. If you are anxious, you will likely convey that anxiety to your child, and any undue tension can hinder test performance.

Most schools that use standardized testing send the results home to the parents. When you receive your child's scores, read the directions carefully to learn how to interpret them. If you have questions about the different numbers, ask the school principal to explain them. Don't be embarrassed or intimidated. Teachers often get their own crash course in deciphering the code each year.

If your school doesn't send the results home, and you would like to know how your child fared, call the principal. If the test booklet becomes part of your child's school records, you are permitted by law to view it.

You may feel that the results accurately reflect what you know about your child. However, if you feel there is a discrepancy between how your child performs in the classroom and how she performed on the test, speak to her teacher. Ask whether the results of the test are consistent with your child's performance. Keep in mind that many circumstances can affect test results. If your child didn't feel well, was unable to concentrate, or incorrectly interpreted the directions, the results will not be valid. If the teacher agrees that the test results are grossly inconsistent, and if the test results affect your child's education (determining reading or math group, for instance), you may request that your child take the test again. Testing companies can and will provide alternative tests.

Standardized tests can be useful to schools, teachers, and parents, but they can also be misused. Sometimes this limited—and yes, flawed—form of measurement is used to determine whether a child should be promoted or retained, whether a child qualifies for special services, whether a teacher is successful, and whether a school system deserves to receive funds. But a standardized test should never be the sole basis of an important educational decision, particularly one that will affect individual children. Observational data and assessment of the child's teacher, parents, and sometimes specialists, should also be considered.

Observing Your Child in the Classroom

Undoubtedly the best way to collect information about your child's school experience is to observe the class in action. You may want to observe for a crucial hour, a morning, or a full day. With advance notice, most schools welcome parent observers. Send a note to your child's teacher (*not* the principal) first. Explain that you are working with your child at home and would like to learn more about the curriculum and her teaching methods. By watching, you'll be able to help your child in a way that is consistent with what the teacher is doing. Don't be shy about offering to help as well as observe—the more direct contact you have with the children, the better. Keep in mind that not every day is necessarily a good time to observe. The children may be at gym or participating in a special event. Also, most teachers would prefer you not come in September, when classroom routines and rules are just being established. Be aware, as well, that your child may not behave the same way while you are observing as he would if you were not present.

If possible, volunteer to help out in your child's classroom on a regular basis. Being a regular visitor will allow you, your child's teacher, and your child to relax into more normal behavior. Take your cues from the teacher, and try not to offer suggestions too often. Let the teacher know how much you enjoy being in the classroom. If a concern arises, schedule a conference to talk with the teacher just as you would if you were not working side by side.

Even if you can't come in to school once a week, offer to go along on a field trip or to help out with a special project. As you work with your child's classmates, you will discover a great deal about how children learn at this grade level and you'll learn more about the academic goals. Your child will see firsthand how much you value education. His pride in your participation will go a long way toward helping him succeed in school.

Appendixes

Homonym Pairs*

red / read	sent / cent	sale / sail
blew / blue	knew / new	where / wear
write / right	hear / here	week / weak
your / you're	threw / through	our / hour
know / no	eye / I	two / too
meat / meet	by / buy	whole / hole

*These are sometimes called homophones, with the word "homonym" being reserved for words that look and sound the same: for example, bear (the animal) and bear (the verb).

Frequently Misspelled Words

about
across
again
almost
also
always
another
answer
any
anyone
are
beautiful
because
been
before
beginning
believe
built
busy

buy
country
does
done
early
enough
especially
everybody
everyone
except
excited
favorite
February
first
friends
getting
guess
have
hear

heard
knew
know
laugh
lose
meant
myself
new
none
often
our
particular
people
probably
ready
really
right
said
school

separate
something
sometimes
terrible
their
then
thought
trouble
until
used
usually
very
wear
Wednesday
were
women
would

Index

books (cont.)
    fiction, see fiction; novels
    "how to," 74
    joke and riddle, 73
    letters in, 108
    math, 135, 141, 173, 179
    middle grade novels, 71
    nonfiction, see nonfiction books; reference
        books
    picture, 66–67, 70, 92
    poetry, 113
    recognition and use of different parts of,
        96, 99–100
    selection of, 70, 113
    series, 69–70
brainstorming, 114, 115, 116
But So game, 78
But That's Another Story (Asher), 133

C

calculators, in math exercises, 142–43, 149, 185
calendars, 29, 156–57, 162, 220
    making of, 160
    in math assessment, 51, 60
capacity, 49–50, 60, 157–58
CAPS, 86
card catalog, 96
card games, fraction war, 187
Carroll, Lewis, 84
Castles (McCauley), 74
cause-and-effect relationships, determining of,
    75, 78
CD-ROMs, encyclopedias on, 74, 98
chapter books, 71
    read-aloud, 68
    short, 70
character charts, 81
character sketches, 80–81
Charlotte's Web (White), 86
charts, making of, 99–101, 128
chess playing, 80, 139
cinquains, writing of, 113
classroom observations, 197
codes:
    homonyms in, 93
    secret, 25
Cohen, Neil, 149
coin tossing, 173
collections:
    alphabetizing items in, 97
    multiplication and, 152
    organization of, 24
    synonyms for, 92
comics, 67, 72, 77

communication:
    dramatic, 25
    reading aloud as, 66
    writing as, 104–17
compare and contrast, 75, 81–83
    assessment of knowledge of, 39, 57
competition, 35
compound words, 87, 94
    assessment of knowledge of, 40, 57
computer catalogs, 96
computers, 66, 69, 98
    CD-ROM encyclopedia for, 74, 98
    Internet use and, 74–75, 115
    revision with, 117
    spreadsheets for, 187
conclusions, drawing, 75, 79–81
    assessment of, 39, 57
conferences, parent-teacher, 189–93
confidence, 18–19, 21, 26, 34
    in writing, 43, 111, 112, 120
congruency, 167
context clues, use of, 57, 75, 83–84
    tips for, 83
contractions, spelling of, 124
conversations, thoughtful, 88
cooperation, 22
creativity, 24
    of parents, 18
    of third graders, 18–19, 26
criticism:
    self-, 22
    sensitivity to, 21
crossword puzzles, 87, 125
    homonyms in, 94
cultural awareness, 23
cursive writing, 43, 58, 128–29
    difficulties with, 128–29
Cushman, Jean, 173

D

daily reading, encouraging of, 65, 69–72
data, recording of, 176
daughters, books clubs for, 72
debates, 82–83
decimal system, 147
details, supporting, 41, 58, 86
    in paragraphs, 43
developmental overview, 20–26
    cultural awareness in, 23
    flightiness in, 24–25
    hardiness and impulsiveness in, 24
    new dimension in, 20–21
    relationships in, 21–22
Dewey decimal system, 96

Activity Pages

What a Morning !

Running helped build my appetite. I ate three bowls of cereal.

Cramming my lunch and my books into my backpack wasn't easy.

Aah! I looked at the light on my pillow. I had overslept!

After I tied my sneakers, I ran downstairs for breakfast.

"Luke," said my brother, "you forgot your homework." He handed it to me just as I was about to zip my backpack up.

"Catch you later!" I called back, and I sped down the driveway.

Know what I need? I thought as I stepped on the bus.

Luckily, I jumped out of bed and got dressed quick.

Mom said, "That's enough. You'd better pack up your stuff."

"Open wide," said my mother. She popped a vitamin into my mouth as I ran out the door.

Time Line

Write dates at the top and use the boxes below to tell what happened.

Story Map

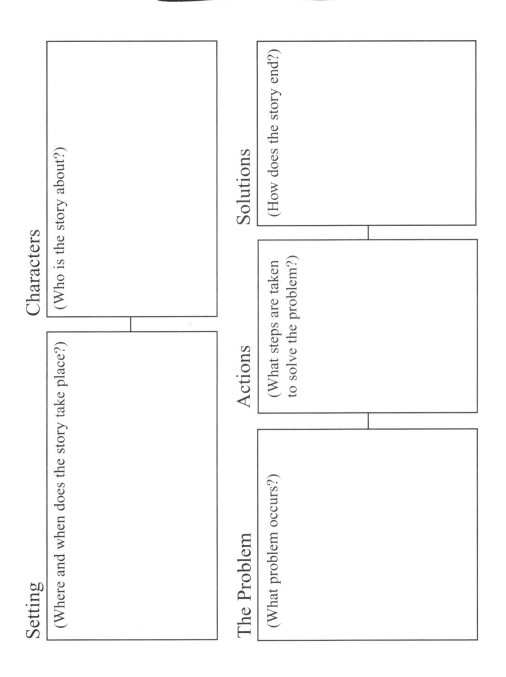

Characters
(Who is the story about?)

Setting
(Where and when does the story take place?)

Solutions
(How does the story end?)

Actions
(What steps are taken to solve the problem?)

The Problem
(What problem occurs?)

Editor's Checklist

	Date	Date	Date
Does the story make sense?			
Capital letters at the beginning of sentences?			
Capital letters in names of people or places?			
Punctuation at the end of each sentence? (.?!)			
Quotation marks (" ") around dialogue?			
Spelling checked?			

(to be used at the end of the third-grade year)

Editor's Checklist

	Date	Date	Date
Does the story make sense?			
Capital letters at the beginning of sentences?			
Capital letters in names of people or places?			
Punctuation at the end of each sentence? (.?!)			
Quotation marks (" ") around dialogue?			
Do sentences run on and on?			
Each new paragraph indented?			
Spelling checked?			

Attribute Shapes

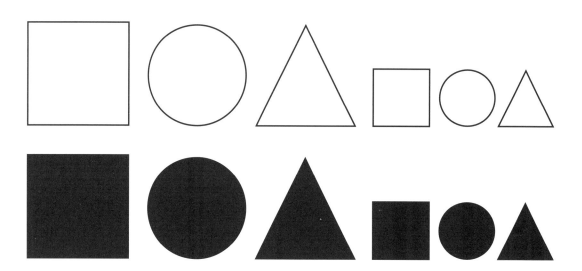

Small	Triangle	Not circle
Large	Not small	Not triangle
Square	Not large	Black
Circle	Not square	White

Multiplication Table

x	1	2	3	4	5	6	7	8	9	10
1										
2										
3										
4										
5										
6										
7										
8										
9										
10										

Calendar Page

Sunday	Monday	Tuesday	Wednesday	Thursday	Friday	Saturday

Pattern Block Template

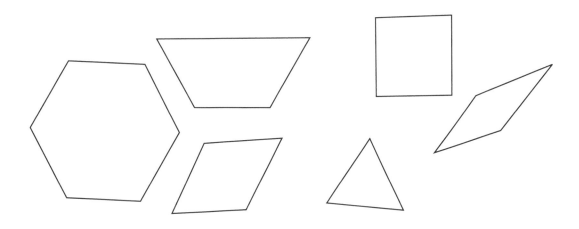

Quadrilateral	Polygon	Hexagon
Not quadrilateral	Regular polygon	Not hexagon
Has parallel edges	Has no parallel edges	Not polygon